Listening In

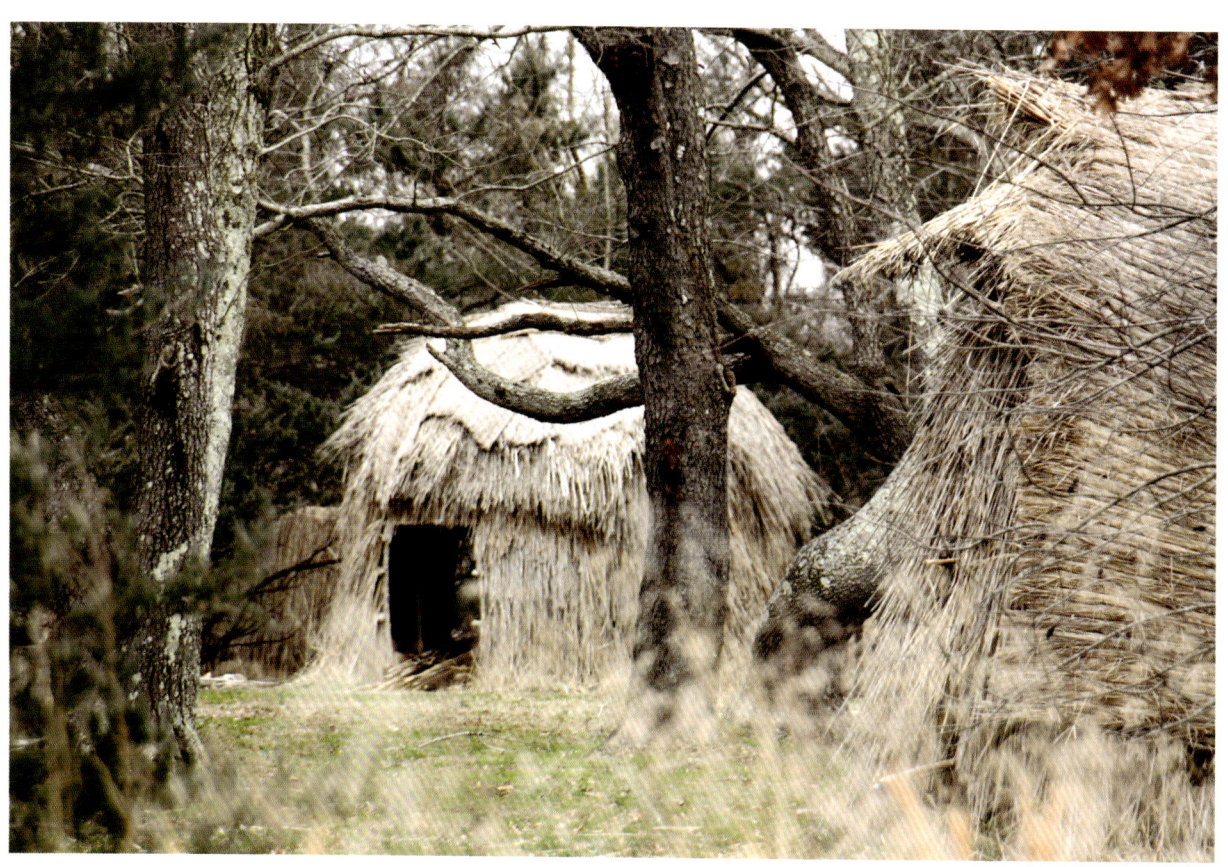

A reconstructed Woodland Indian hamlet at Historic St. Mary's City.

Listening In

Echoes and Artifacts
from Maryland's Mother County

Photographs and Stories
by Merideth M. Taylor

with a poem by Lucille Clifton and
a foreword by Jeffrey Hammond

George F. Thompson Publishing
in association with Passager

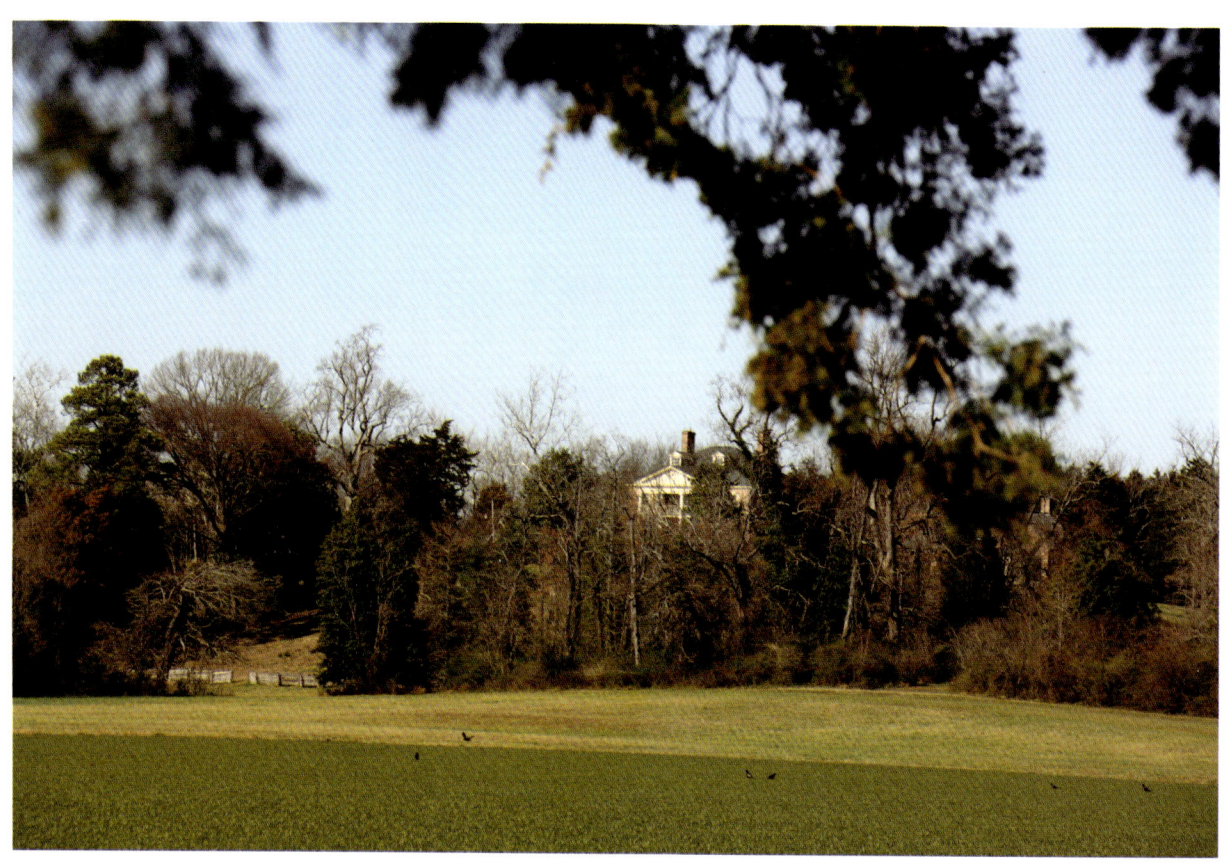

The front of historic Mulberry Fields (ca. 1755) faces the Potomac River.

For the citizens of
St. Mary's County

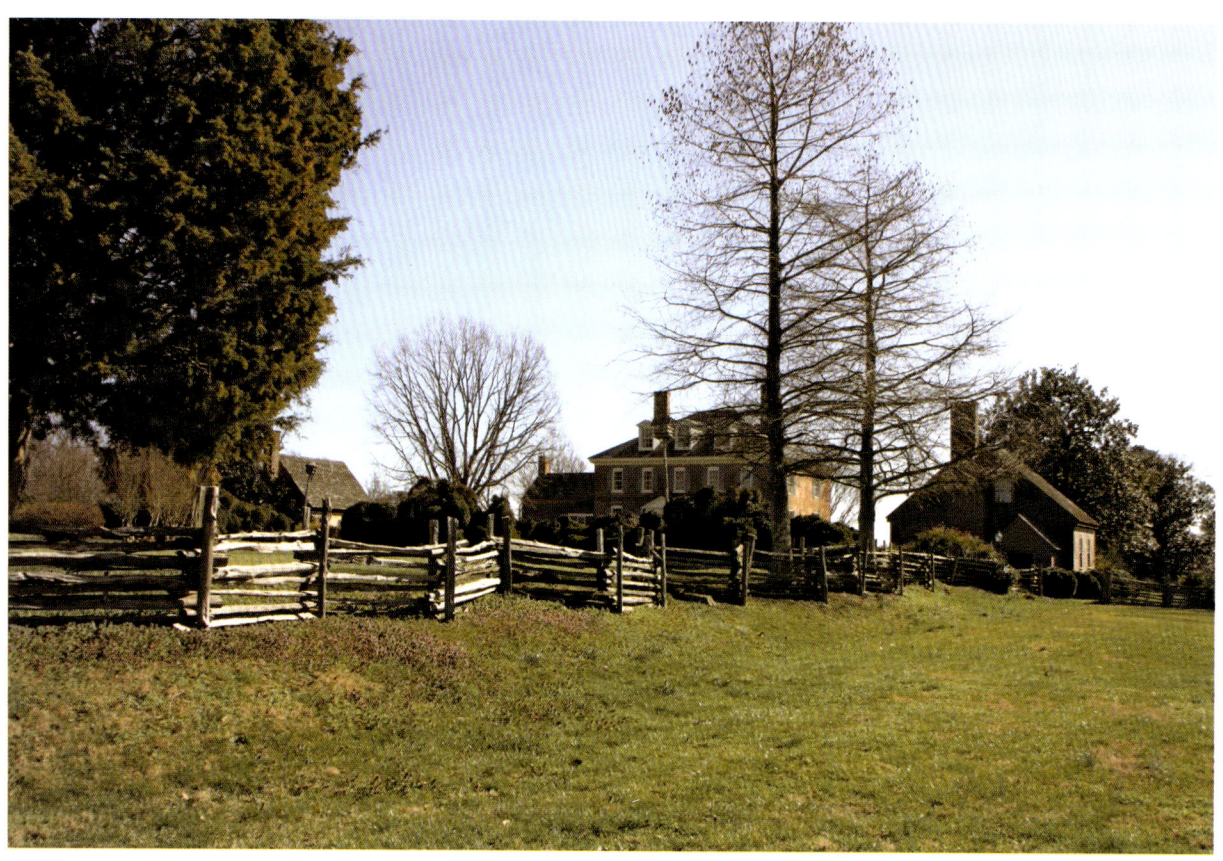

The back of historic Mulberry Fields in Beauvue.

mulberry fields

they thought the field was wasting
and so they gathered the marker rocks and stones and
piled them into a barn   they say that the rocks were shaped
some of them scratched with triangles and other forms   they
must have been trying to invent some new language they say
the rocks went to build that wall there guarding the manor and
some few were used for the state house
crops refused to grow
i say the stones marked an old tongue and it was called eternity
and pointed toward the river   i say that after that collection
no pillow in the big house dreamed   i say that somewhere under
here moulders one called alice whose great grandson is old now
too and refuses to talk about slavery   i say that at the
masters table only one plate is set for supper   i say no seed
can flourish on this ground once planted then forsaken   wild
berries warm a field of bones
bloom how you must I say

—Lucille Clifton (2004)

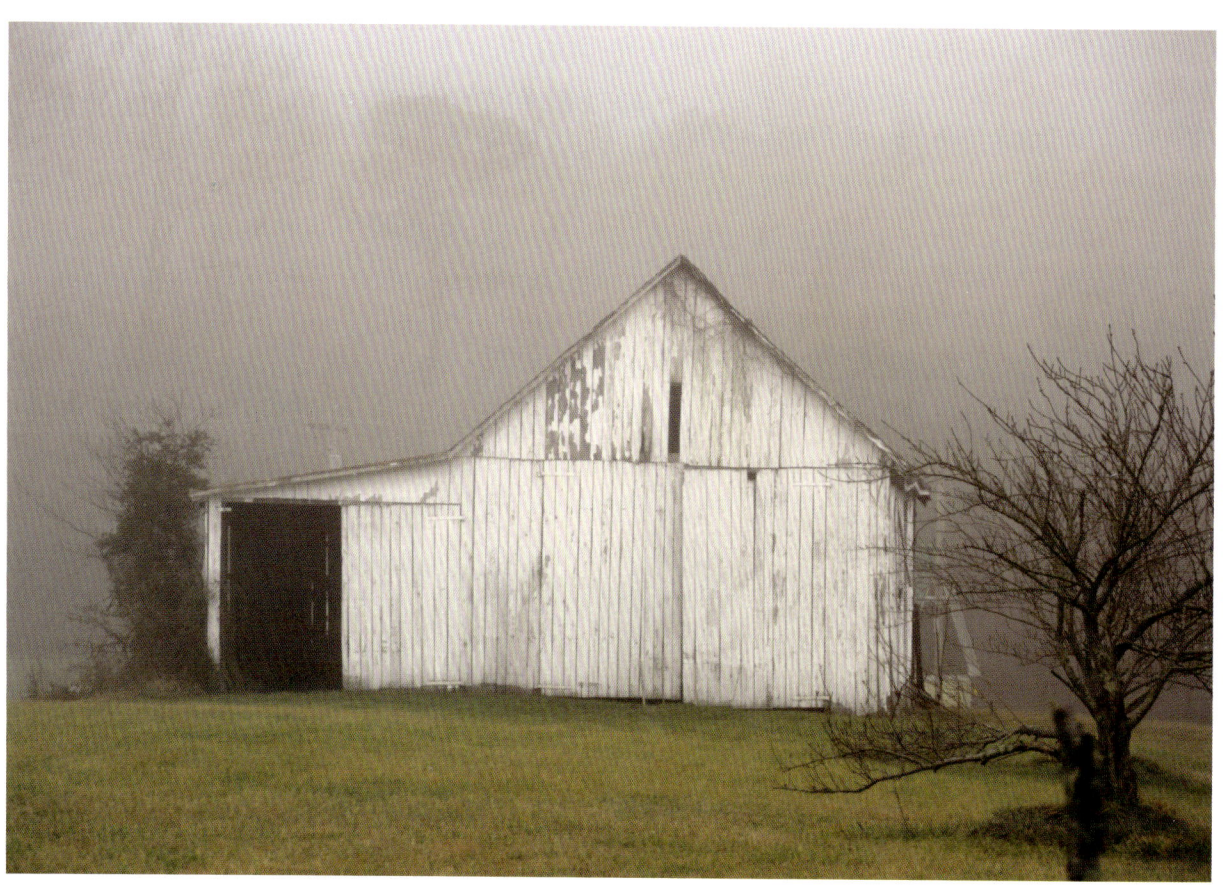

Tobacco barn on Point Lookout Road.

Foreword

*L*istening In documents a landscape that my colleague, Merideth Taylor, knows well and loves deeply. Through a dynamic interplay of striking photographs and evocative prose, she presents St. Mary's County in southern Maryland as a haunting palimpsest revealing multiple traces of human experience through time.

Along the way, Taylor reminds us of the fluidity of the places that we encounter, inhabit, and remember. Landscapes encompass everything that has occurred there: To observe them closely is to see through time as well as space. What we confront at the moment of seeing is always a still from a moving picture that began long before we were there—and, as *Listening In* beautifully illustrates, what is no longer there is as powerful as what remains.

Listening In presents fictive reconstructions of the bygone voices of southern Maryland. While these voices remind us of our own impermanence, they also assert the powerful continuities that unite us with those who have preceded us in the places where we live. By removing the usual barrier between the present observer and the observed past, Merideth Taylor avoids the easy sentimentality that often arises when we confront earlier times and places. As a photographer, she records the exteriors of old structures; as a writer, she engages us with imagined embodiments of the people who once inhabited and animated them. As *Listening In* amply demonstrates, art always finds a way inside.

JEFFREY HAMMOND
*George B. and Willma Reeves Distinguished Professor in the Liberal Arts
and Professor of English, St. Mary's College of Maryland*

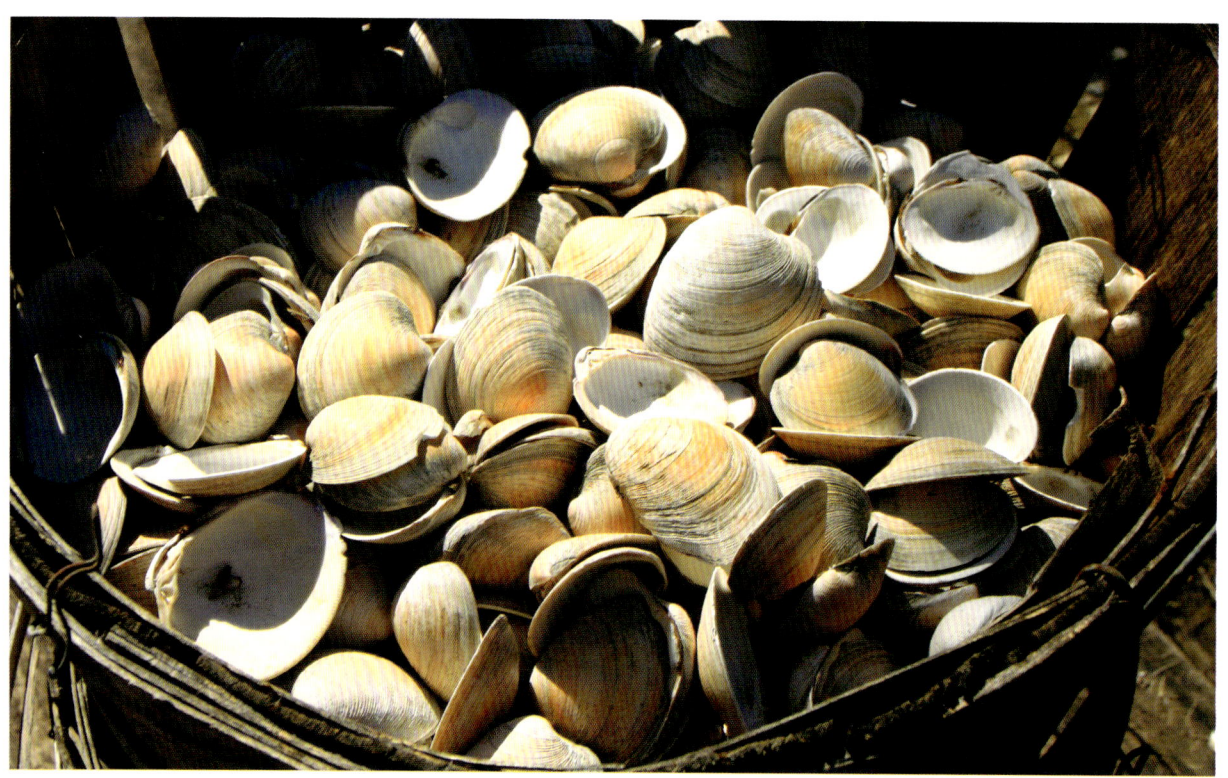

Chesapeake Bay clams.

Introduction

WHEN DID I START "LISTENING IN" to the past of my community? The genesis of this project may actually have been in childhood when I walked through my neighborhood in Denver, Colorado, looking into house windows with curiosity about the lives of the inhabitants. Especially on winter evenings when lights would come on early, I would imagine a coziness around a family hearth, though I knew even then that the reality of what was going on inside those houses may have been anything but warm and cozy. I felt both lonely and liberated by my "outsider" status. Lonely because I longed for connection and liberated because I was free to imagine.

Educational and career choices further shaped and developed my interest in the connections of houses and other structures with their inhabitants and stories. As a dancer and actor, I benefitted from learning to empathize with others. As a theater director and choreographer, I learned to think in images. As a playwright and collector of oral histories, I learned to listen to people talk and learned that, as folklorists Michael and Carrie Kline taught me, listening can be an act of love.

I am lucky to have lived in many places, mostly in the United States, and have learned to appreciate them all. I have had the privilege of insulating myself more than most from environmental toxins, crime, and poverty. Still, even this relatively peaceful county in the southern Chesapeake region that I happily call home is rapidly transitioning from rural to suburban, and it has all the environmental challenges, problems, and cultural shifts one would expect in a burgeoning population. As with any great economic shift, ways of life change, and people do not benefit equally from the changes.

The earliest and most dramatic shift was experienced by the indigenous peoples who had made their homes in this area for thousands of years before colonists arrived to claim and "settle" the land. Early in the seventeenth century, the Calvert family, wealthy Catholics in Protestant-ruled England, were granted a charter to the land that is now the state of Maryland. In 1633, Leonard Calvert and a group of adventurers sailed forth on the ships *Ark* and *Dove* to establish the first settlement and new capital of the colony. They named their capital St. Mary's City to honor the Virgin Mary and issued a proclamation extending freedom of worship to all Christians. With this radical act, the colony established its reputation as the American birthplace of the values of religious tolerance and separation of church and state. Recognized as a National Historic Landmark in 1969, St. Mary's City is the best preserved founding site of a seventeenth-century English colony in North America. Now a living-history museum, Historic St. Mary's City sits alongside St. Mary's College of Maryland on a peninsula bordered by the Potomac and Patuxent Rivers and Chesapeake Bay.

The shift from woodland to tobacco plantations during the seventeenth century was swift and seismic in its impact on the peoples and land. But once colonial culture became dominant and the transition to commercial agriculture and water culture was made, the pace of life in St. Mary's County slowed. Political upheaval in 1694 resulted in removal of the Maryland capital to Annapolis, and the area began to earn its long-held reputation as a rural "backwater."

Despite fluctuating tobacco prices, war-time attacks by the British in 1776 and 1814, "oyster wars" between Maryland and Virginia watermen, emancipation of Maryland's enslaved in 1864, and economic devastation in the wake of the Civil War, the county was a place marked by tradition and continuity. Significant change arrived with World War II and the establishment of the Patuxent River Naval Air Station. As job opportunities increased, the population grew and became more diverse. Not all of the changes were positive, and many things that would have been better changed did not. A stark divide between rich and poor remained. As the military became the economic engine and agriculture, oystering, and crabbing declined, real estate taxes increased. Many of the people who lived on the water and made their living from farming and fishing lost their land. Not surprisingly, with a past steeped in slavery and segregation, attitudes and enmities between black and white countians can still be felt more than 150 years after the Civil War and more than fifty years after the Voting Rights Act of 1965.

The images and stories in this book are by no means a full representation of the history and cultures of the area. The collection grew out of exploring county roads and learning the history of the community and southern Maryland. It is a work of imagination inspired by what I have observed and learned since arriving in 1990 to teach theater and dance at St. Mary's College of Maryland. As I explored St. Mary's and neighboring counties, I found the uniqueness of the rural, owner-built homes much more interesting and aesthetically appealing than the mass-produced homes sprouting up in former tobacco fields. The tobacco buyout during the late 1990s insured the demise of 300 years of tobacco culture in southern Maryland. As housing developments replaced crops, I was sad to see the rural landscape disappearing.

Over the decades, I watched and recorded the slow deterioration of abandoned structures and became fascinated with nature's process of reclamation. The buildings were gradually devoured by the very plant life that had been displaced to make way for human habitation. No doubt my own process of aging provided me with a sense of identity and empathy, as if the structures were characters I had known. I began to see the buildings' gradual collapse and, in many cases, disappearance altogether as metaphors for the passing of time and fading of a way of life.

After years of photographing the landscape and its buildings, I began to imagine bits of dialogue, snippets of conversation that could have taken place in the houses and places of business. Like verbal snapshots of life lived in the buildings. I first called these "ghost voices," thinking of them as echoes or reverberations of what I might have heard standing outside a building with my camera listening in. Although the stories that accompany the photographs are based on reading about the area's history and many years of conducting and editing local oral histories, they are fictional and are not intended to reflect in any way on actual residents or occupants. My hope, nevertheless, is that, in these imagined moments, there is a respectful and truthful history of a community and people I have grown to love.

Listening In

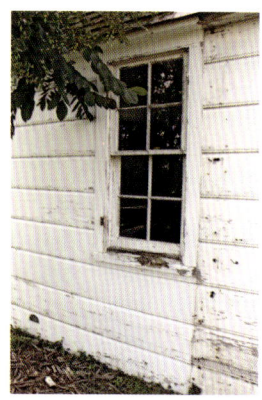

Awake, my soul, and with the sun
Thy daily stage of duty run;
Shake off dull sloth, and joyful rise,
To pay thy morning sacrifice.

—BISHOP THOMAS KEN (1709)

TURNING AWAY FROM THE SCHOOLHOUSE WINDOW, the boy slid down the rough wall to sit with his back against the clapboard. He tilted his head to one side listening intently, his brown skin still beaded with sweat. He had been up early fetching wood and water and sweeping out the school-room, readying it for the students who now occupied it. He sang along quietly, as the children on the other side of the wall joined their teacher in the morning hymn. The boy sat here whenever he could, memorizing the recitations of grammar and sums, incantations he thought might prove useful to him somehow. But it was the songs he loved, and his fingers would move as he listened, already feeling the banjo in his hand.

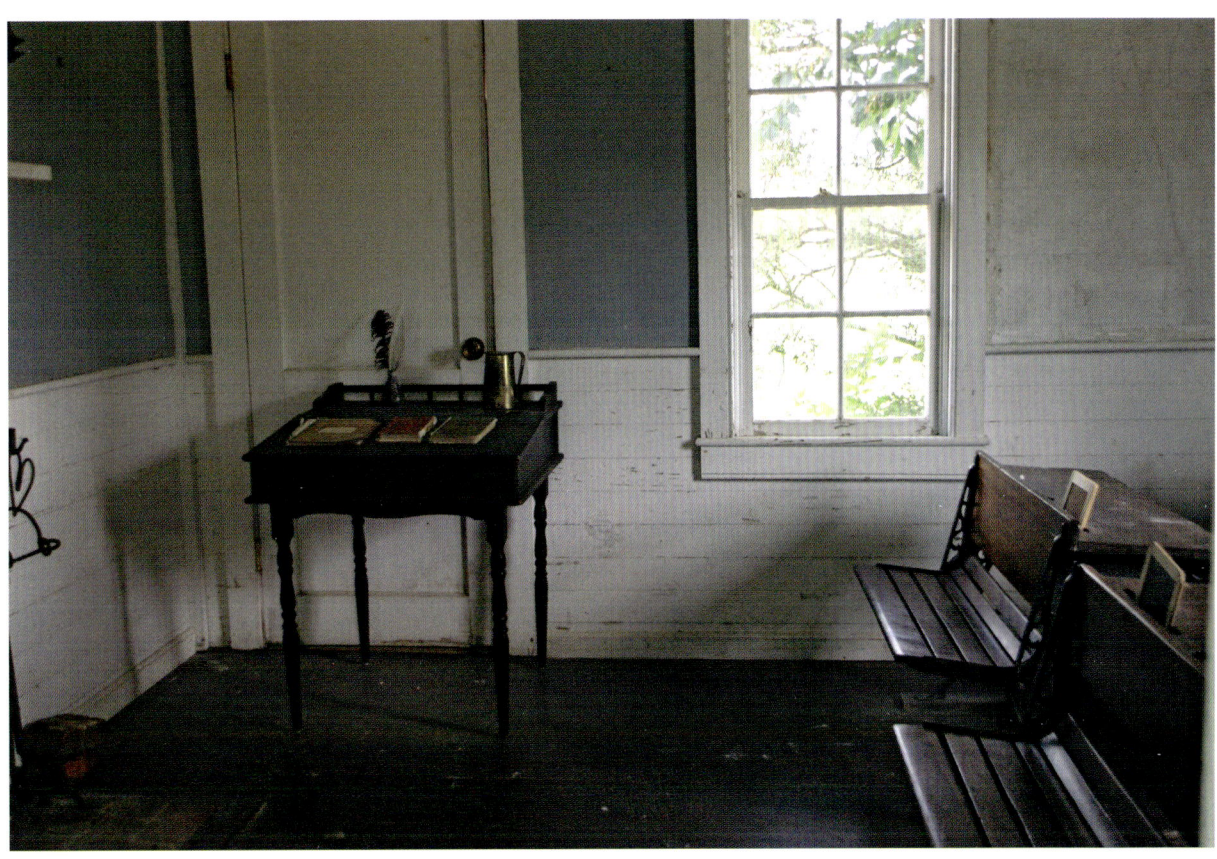

Schoolhouse on Sotterley Plantation (ca.1703) in Hollywood.

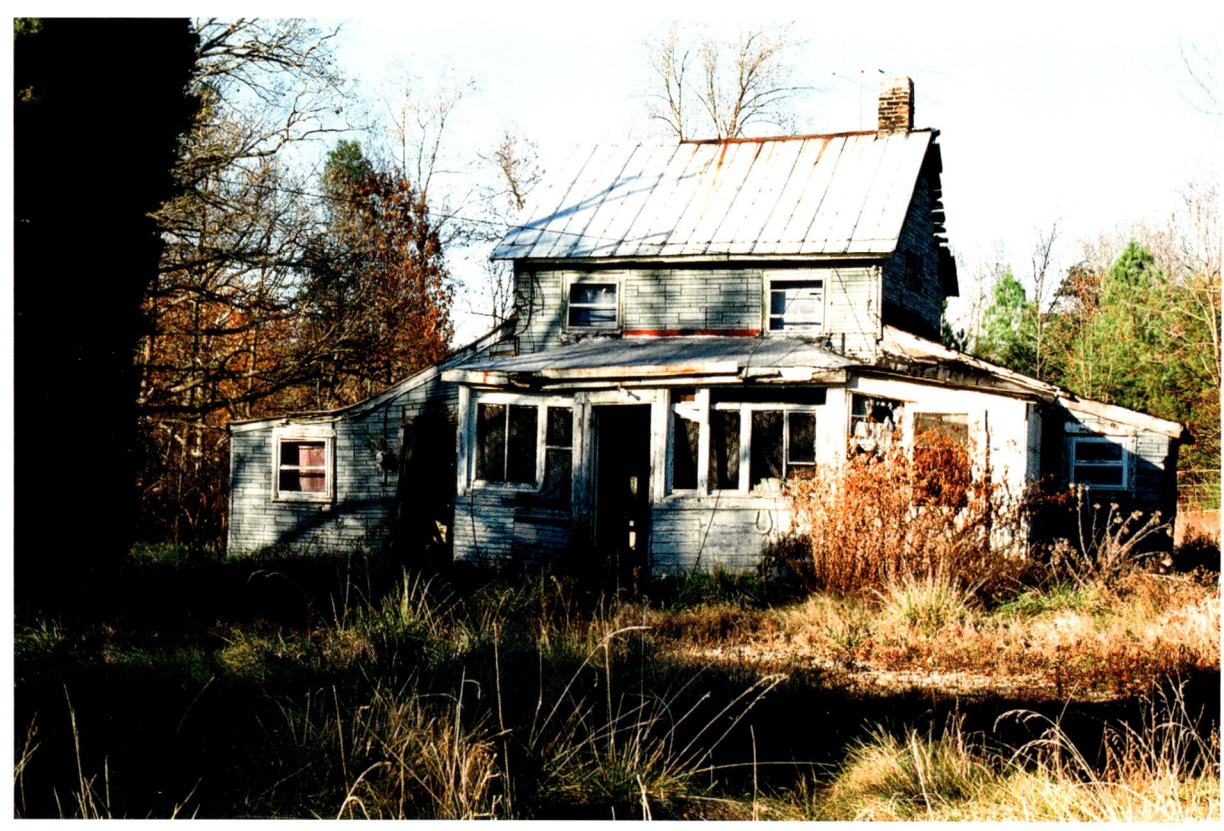

Drayden area.

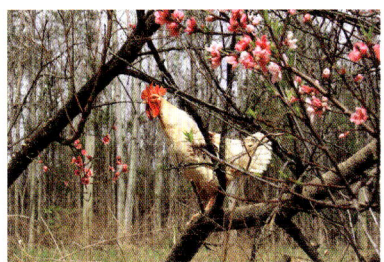

Come on to the table everyone. Eat every bit of that up,
and drink some more water. That'll fill you up.

GROWING UP ON A FARM BY CHESAPEAKE BAY, life was hard, but the family had good times, too. They were sharecroppers back then and didn't have much. Sometimes, late in the year before the garden was going good, they didn't have much to eat beyond the beans, tomatoes, and pickles the kids helped their mama preserve and the potatoes left in the root cellar. With thirteen kids, that didn't go far. A hog or two meant there was always stuffed ham at Christmas. They had the one milk cow and a few chickens, and the oldest boy would take the eggs and milk to town to buy other things they needed; sugar, molasses, coffee, things like that. He and his brothers would go hunting for squirrels, and the girls would set traps for possum and coons. Their dad wasn't big on hunting or oystering, but he was a hard worker. Every year when tobacco market time came, he'd ride up to Hughesville with Mr. Ford, the farm owner, and come back with a few hundred dollars. He hadn't gone past the fourth grade in school, and the family was never sure whether that money was truly their fair share. But Mr. Ford ended up selling them a little piece of land with their house on it for a price they could afford, so they figured he was basically a fair-minded man. It was hard work, and the family never had money to spend, but they loved each other. They loved being together. And they learned a lot of important lessons about life, about how to stick together and do right by people.

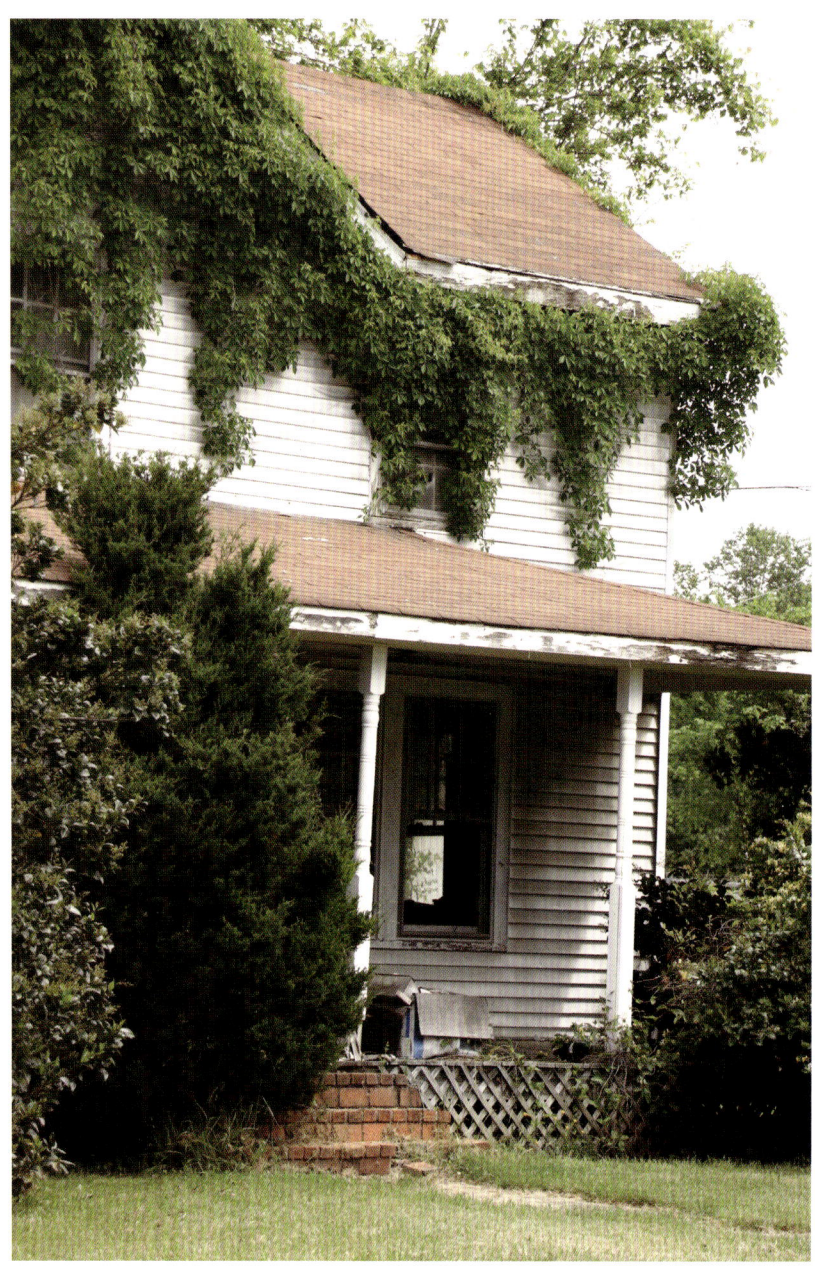

Helen.

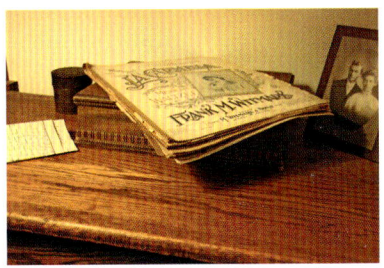

"If you were the only boy in the world and I were the only girl . . ."
Give that letter a rest, Sophie, and come sing with us.

Helen and Josephine sat at the old upright piano, Helen playing the melody and Jo the chords. "*Nothing else would matter in the world today . . .*" The three women often gathered around the piano after the supper dishes were put away. They loved the songs that lifted their spirits and kept their worries at bay. "*We could go on loving in the same old way.*" Sophie had a lovely soprano voice, and together the sisters made a very decent trio. "*I would say such wonderful things to you.*" Jo made a funny face at Sophie, and she finally gave in and joined them. The precious letter left lying on the table had reached her from the front lines in France only three days ago and was already creased with wear from her fingers. "*. . . If you were the only boy in the world and I were the only girl.*" Sophie laughed. "Come on, let's play a rag!" And they launched into "Tiger Rag" with good cheer if not great skill.

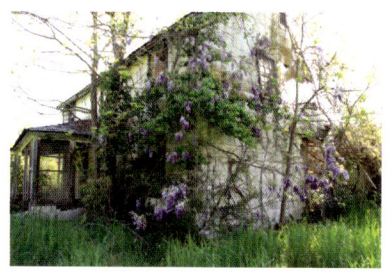

How can there be a bug that color?

OLD MR. STANLEY SAT UNDER HIS GARDEN ARBOR, laden just then with wisteria and old-fashioned roses, and contemplated a bright turquoise-colored beetle the likes of which he had never seen. At least he couldn't remember if he had. It just didn't seem like a color that ought to be in nature. He sat there in the late afternoon sun and marveled at the movement of the beetle's tiny front legs, which seemed to be working the air, but he guessed there must be something there his old eyes couldn't see. He watched it, feeling a momentary kinship, 'til it wandered off, or maybe it was his attention that wandered. He just couldn't get over the beauty of this day. Surely, he thought, this must be the most perfect late-spring day there ever was or maybe ever would be for him.

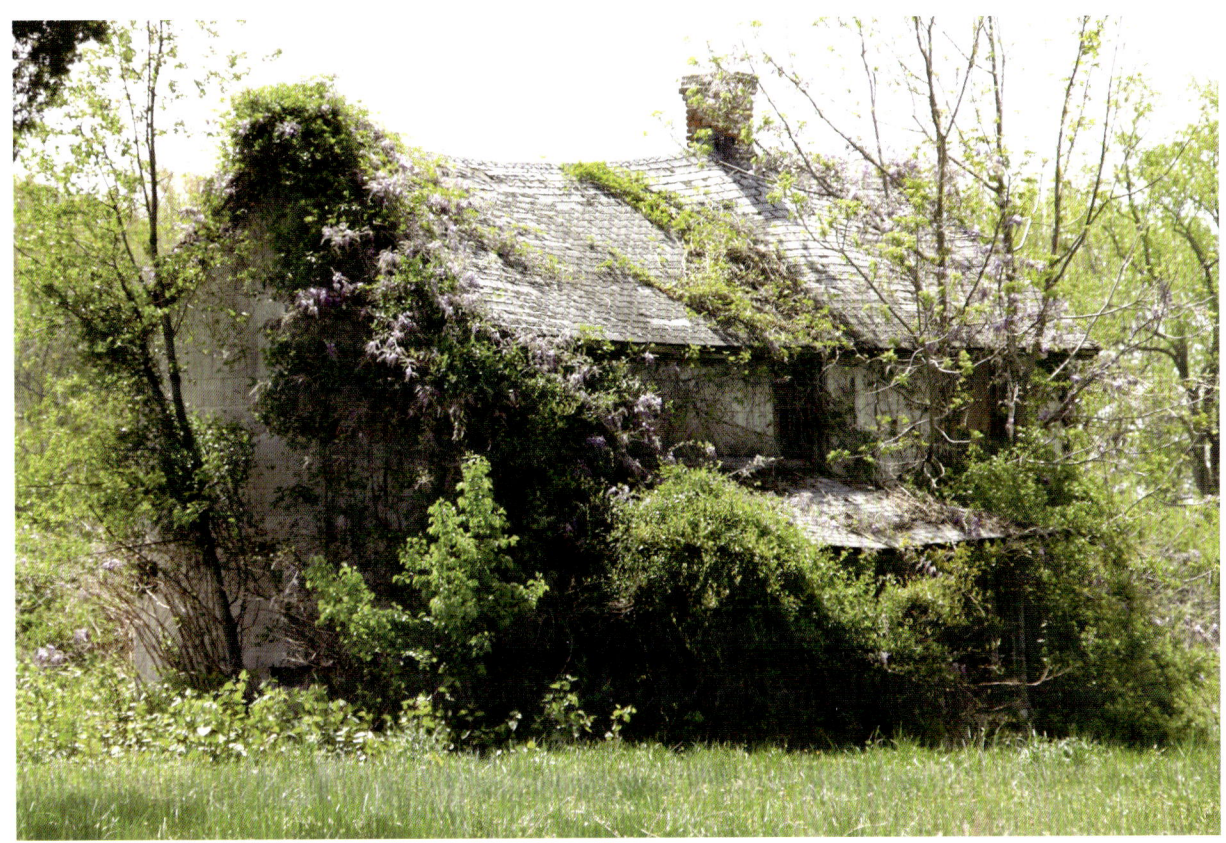

Beachville.

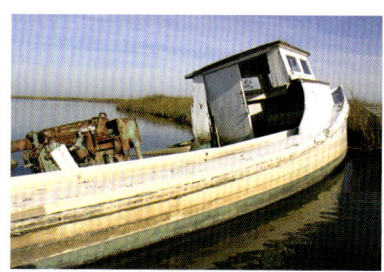

Tonight's the night. Moon should stay hid, but watch out for agents.
A night like this, they're likely to be hiding out in a cove upriver,
listening for motors. Keep it tamped down.

THE TWELVE JUGS OF CORN WHISKEY lined up against the boatshed wall were destined for a ride upriver to Washington. What with the government agents prowling the water and beating down the woods hunting for stills, moonshining was risky business. But so far they'd been lucky. They were making close to 1,400 gallons a week, worth thousands of dollars in the city. No other way they could make that kind of money, not legal anyway. For some folks, Prohibition was just a financial opportunity, and the young fellers appreciated a little excitement in their lives.

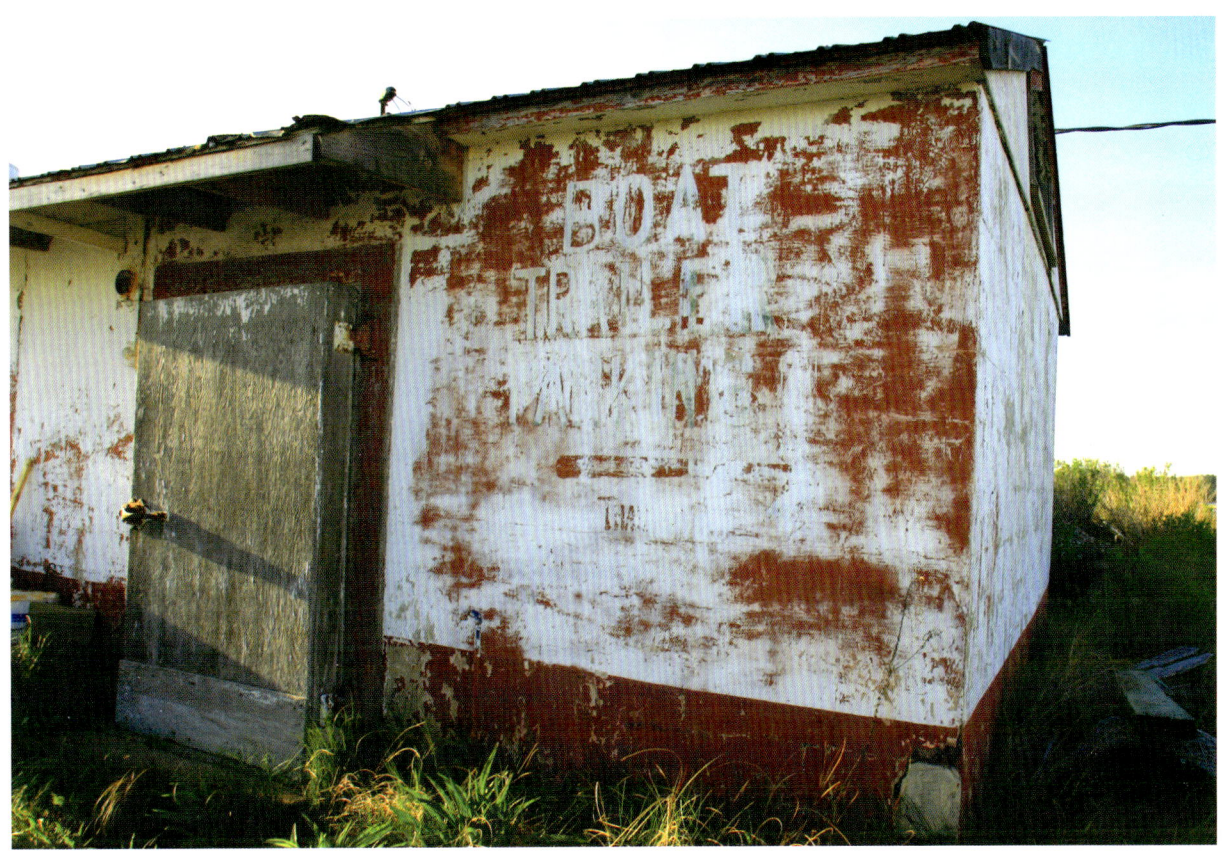

Boat shed on Smith Creek.

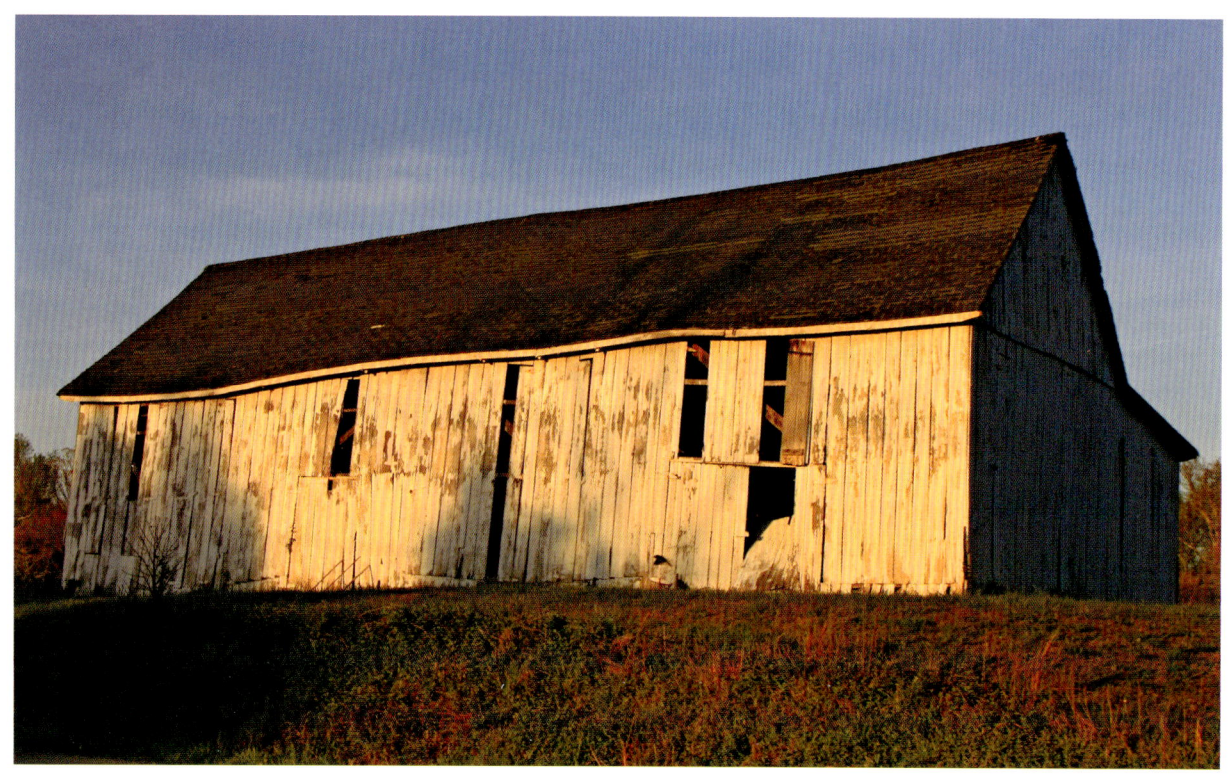

Tobacco barn in Park Hall.

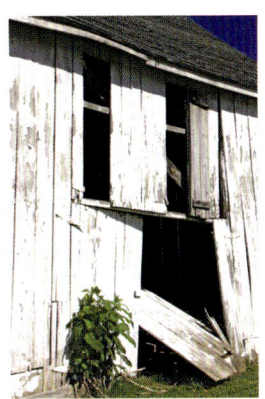

Now you see these? When you get the first three leaves off
the bottom—that's the shaggy stuff—don't let that get in
with your good tobacco. Keep that to itself.

THE THREE SAT THERE TOGETHER STRIPPING THE TOBACCO STALK, mom and sisters. Dad never stripped but the tips. The women did a fine job. When it came to market, buyers said they always knew whose tobacco it was when it was opened up. It had the reputation of the best in the barn. It was work though. Tobacco's hard work, and it's all-year work. Crabbing was good for a while, but they couldn't make it with just what he got on the water. Had to get some land and get that money crop in. Seeding, dropping, weeding, picking off worms, cutting, hanging, put it on sticks, push it off, strip it up into bundles, pack it down, bale it, and hogshead it up. That was the way it was with tobacco.

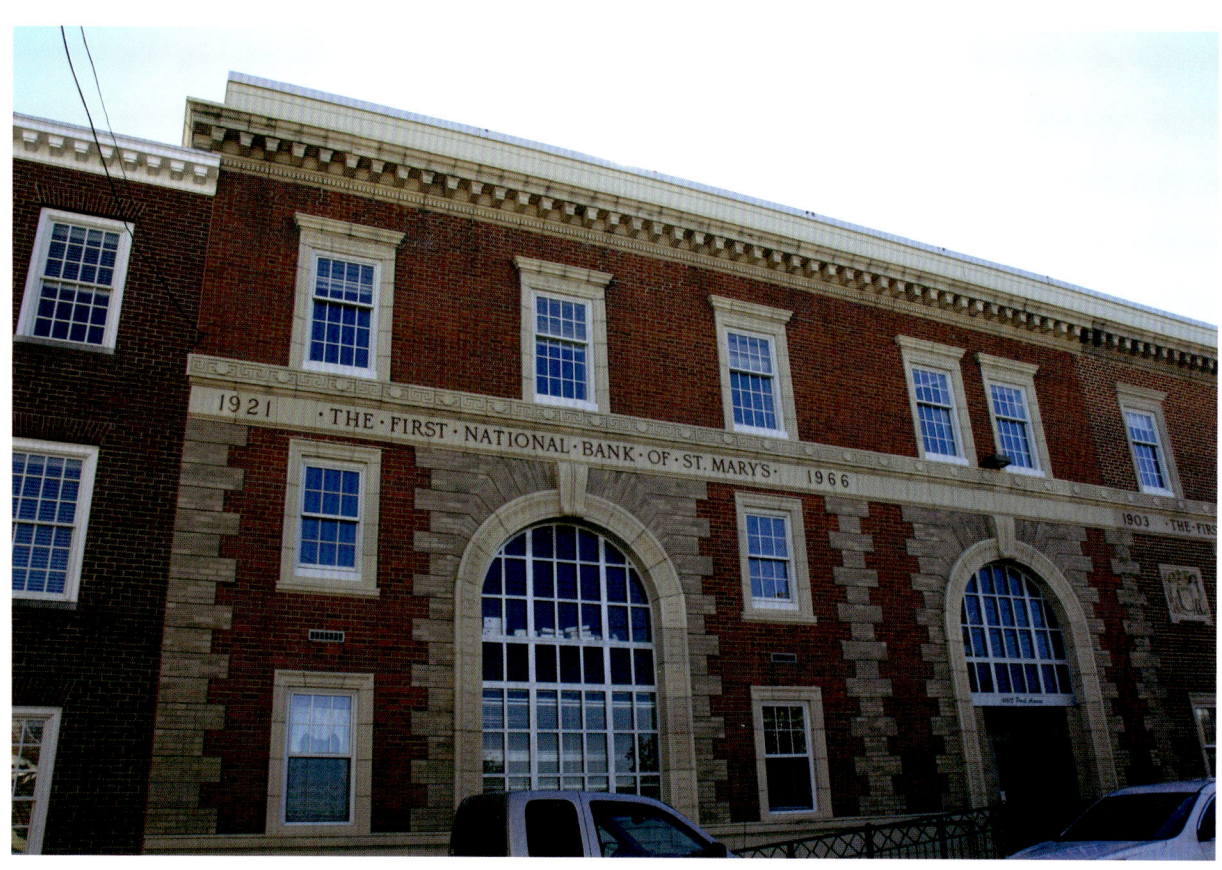

Downtown Leonardtown.

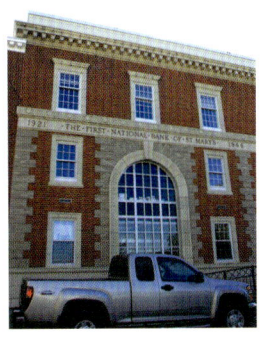

Be done in just a jiffy, Missus.

H IS OLD-MAN FINGERS were just not keeping up with his mind lately. No one upstairs had said anything yet or seemed to notice, least he didn't think so, but he felt it. They called him Uncle George there at the bank, never George or Mr. B. But everyone got on just fine. It had been years now since his janitor job started growing into other jobs as well, mostly in the office, simple chores. He never made any trouble and was trustworthy. When they found out he was a whiz at counting and figures, fast and accurate, they had him doing that every evening as well. He was proud that he could bring home that kind of money to his family. After all, he'd only gone as far as fifth grade. That's how it was when he was coming along. Everybody didn't get to go to school back then. But he was good at numbers, and he had made his own way.

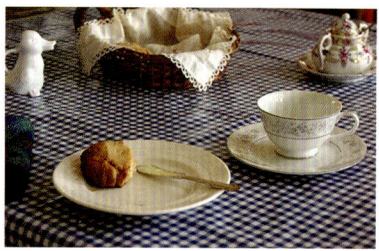

Well, the way I heard it, she was already showing at the wedding…

E LVA PAUSED, holding the Queen of Spades suspended in her hand. "Are you going to play that card or not, Fran? We can't all sit here forever just yackin' about stuff that's none a our business in the first place." The others murmured in half-hearted agreement, except for Sharon who was dying to know the truth of what went on between the couple that had finally gotten them to the alter. The four women met in Millie's kitchen every Thursday, holding their coffee klatch around the big table covered with cheerful, blue-checked oilcloth. Millie always had the coffee going, and they rotated who would bring the cookies, sweet bread, or coffee cake. They were each known for a particular goodie, though Elva had a penchant for experimentation and occasionally would mix it up with something new. Mostly, they talked about people they knew from neighboring farms or church and the foolish or inexplicable things they got up to. Sometimes, scandals involving the rich and famous came into it, and, once in a while, there was real news to discuss. The women weren't always kind to the subjects of their gossip, but most had experienced enough heartbreak in their own lives to temper their opinions with compassion.

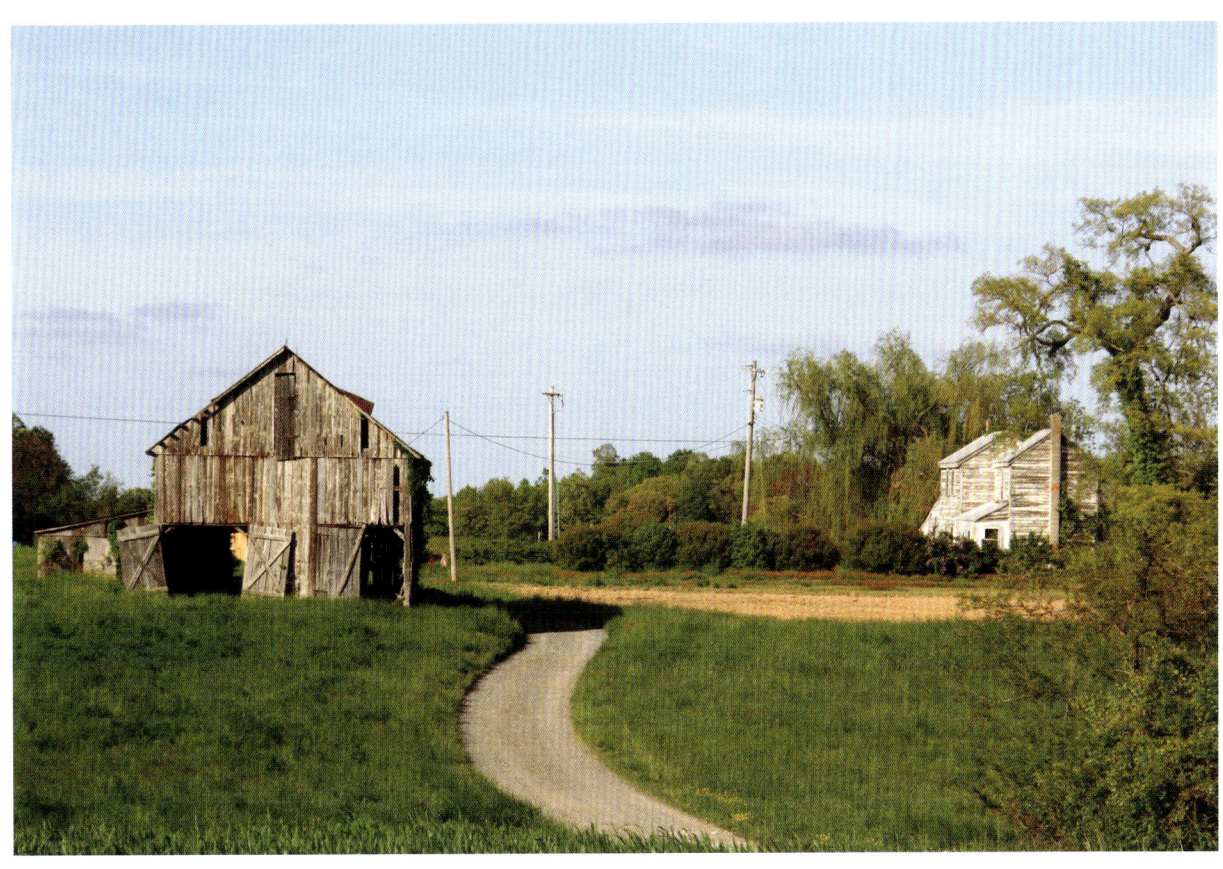

Farm along the Patuxent River.

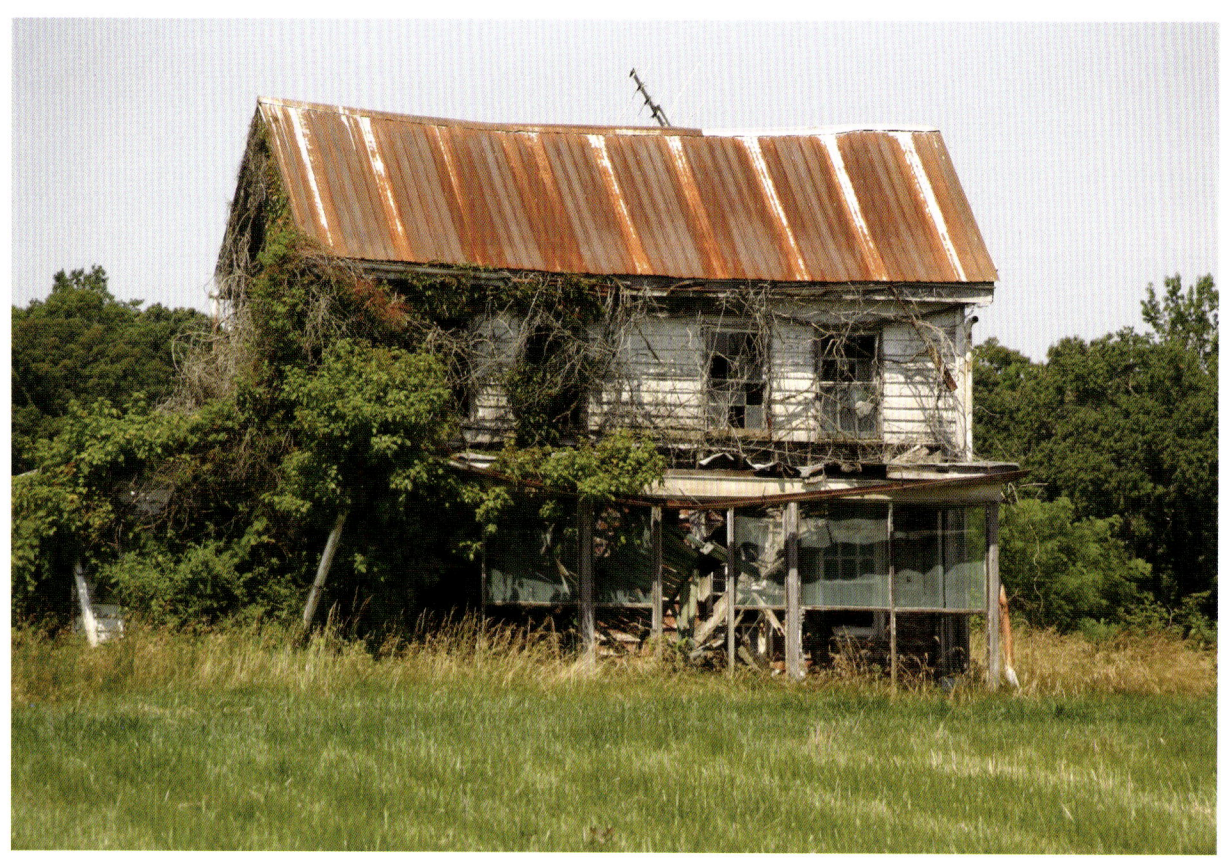

Drayden area.

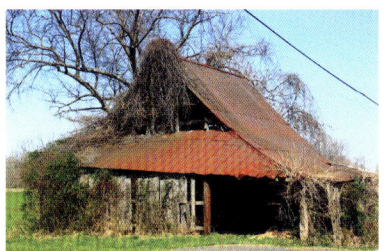

Rise and shine you slug-a-beds! You think them
tobacco worms are sleeping the morning away?
Git yourself up, and get on out to the fields!

P OPS ROUSED THE KIDS SLEEPING FOUR TO A BED with the littlest across
at the foot. It was barely light out, and their lids felt heavy with sleep.
They knew better than to complain, though. There was no tolerance for
whining, and it was likely to lead to a stinging switch across the back of
the legs. These long hot days in the tobacco fields made the kids long for
the school year. Studying and school chores, even the threat of whippings
by Principal Evers, meant salvation from pulling the fat, ugly worms off
the endless rows of tobacco plants. When the turkeys would follow along,
they'd toss them the worms to eat, and that wasn't so bad. The kids were
careful not to miss a worm for fear their Dad might follow through on his
warning that they'd have to eat one as punishment. And then there'd always
be one of the boys who thought it was funny to drop the biggest, greenest
worm down his sister's blouse.

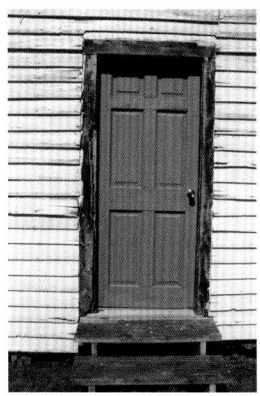

You two take the pail and go on down to the spring while
Frank and Leroy burst some wood for the stove. Girls,
you keep on helping the little ones with their figuring.

TWO OLDER GIRLS WERE BENT OVER the youngest students in their small, scratched, much-repaired desks in the front row, helping them decipher the mysteries of addition and subtraction. The teacher took a couple of eggs and dropped them in the can of water she kept on top of the potbelly stove. A few of the children would go home for lunch, but some who stayed would be glad of a little extra to add to their biscuits and fatback or whatever they brought in their brown bags. The boys might bring back some mulberries from the tree by the well. She turned back to the chalkboard and started putting up the afternoon's lessons, figuring in her head how to make it work for all the different grades.

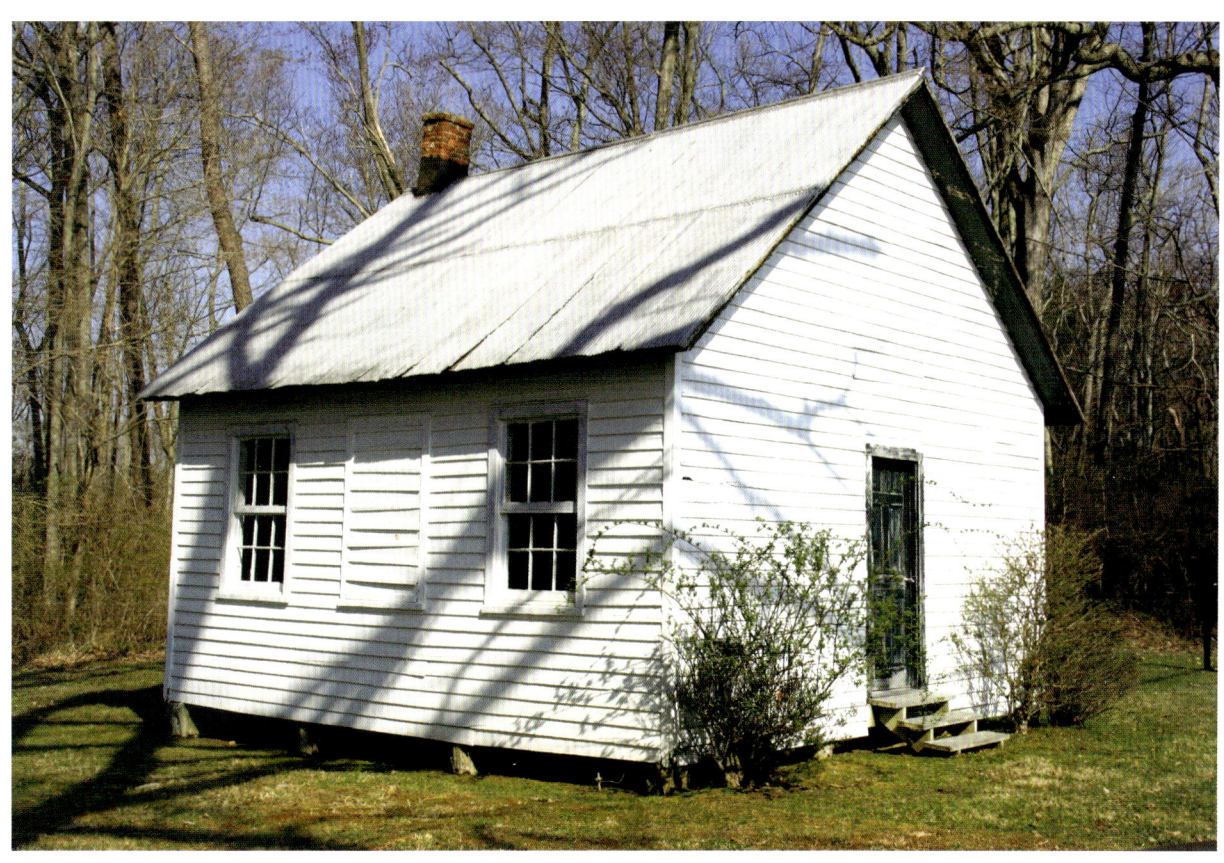

One-room African-American schoolhouse (1890–1944) in Drayden.

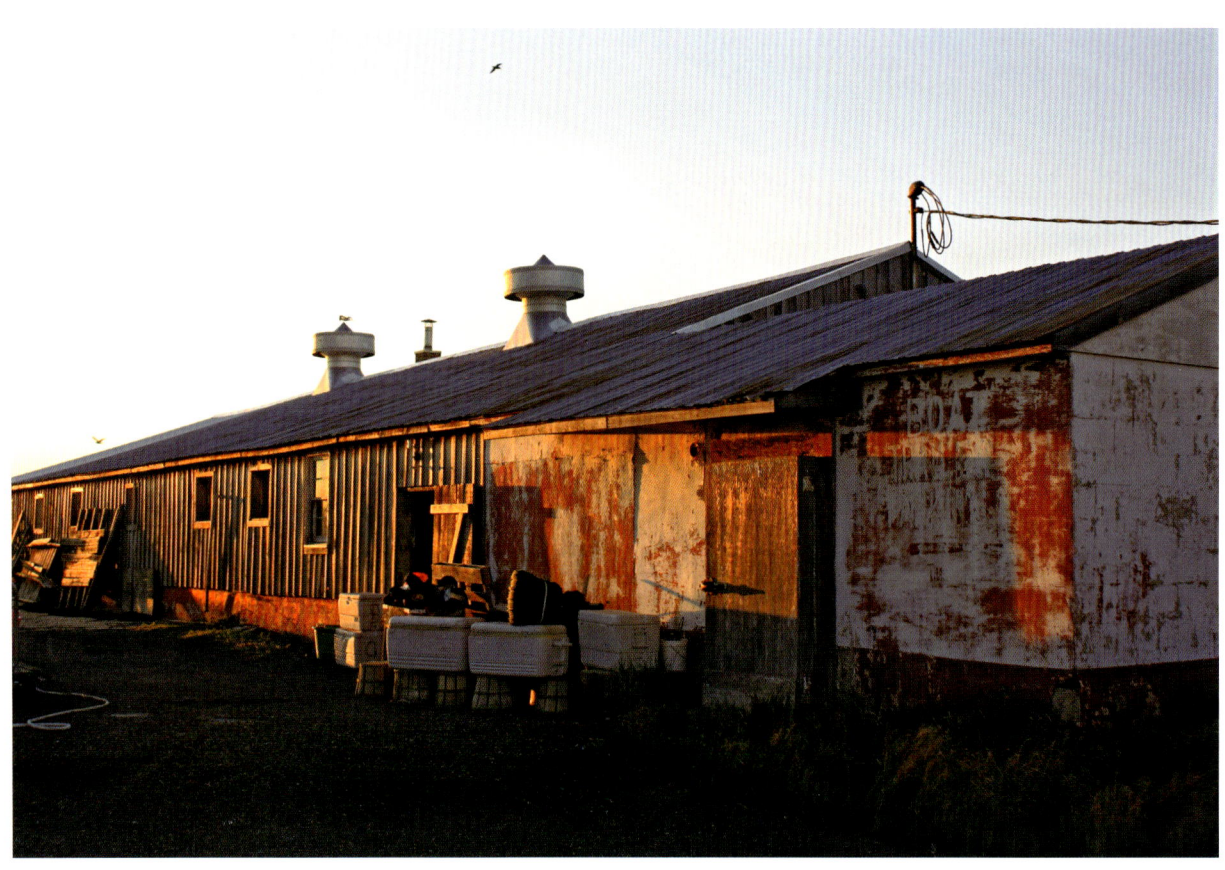

Oyster-shucking house in Wynne.

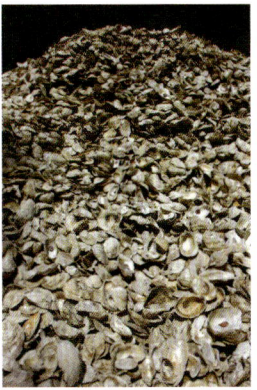

It don't mean a thing if it ain't got that swing . . .

Humming along with someone who was "feeling it" made the time go faster. Shooting the breeze, sharing recipes, that helped, too. The crab pickers were mostly women, the shuckers mostly men except for a few like Thelma. She liked working with her hands, and she was *fast*. Speed was what made a star shucker. When she first started shucking, she got some good hints from Bunton Smith: "Daughter, you got to slip the knife down the bottom shell, *under* the oyster. The way you're going at it, you're cutting right into it, all that liquor running right out." Thelma got it down in no time, knife under, a twist of her wrists, and that was it.

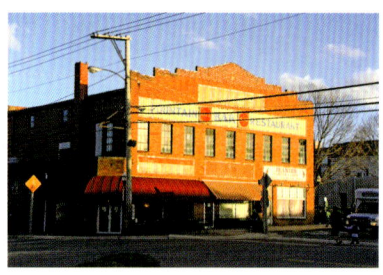

*Ma, if I promise to dress nice and go
to church, can we go to the movie after?*

SUNDAY AFTERNOON MOVIES in town were a family favorite, and the boy had high hopes. He was excited to see the new Disney film, *Fantasia,* playing at Duke's this Sunday. Then again, his sister wanted to see *Pinocchio,* which was playing on Saturday, and she might make fudge to take with them if she got her way. But he figured if he convinced them all to go to *Fantasia,* maybe he'd get a Big Cherry candy bar before they went upstairs to the movie. And if he was *really* lucky, they'd get sodas or at least a pop at the drugstore counter, too. Chances were his mom would say it was too close to supper time, but a guy could always hope. Yes, Sunday! What a day it was going to be.

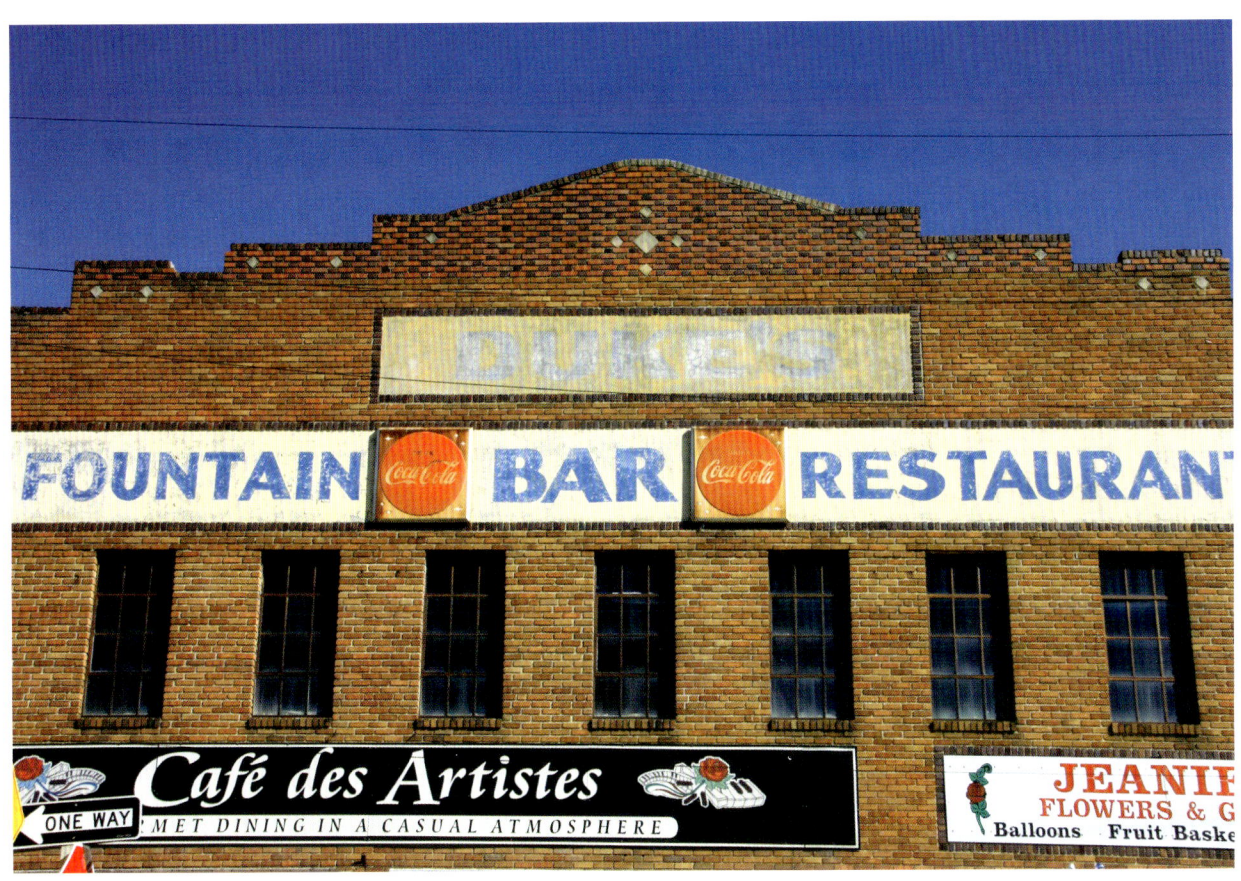

The historic Duke Building in Leonardtown.

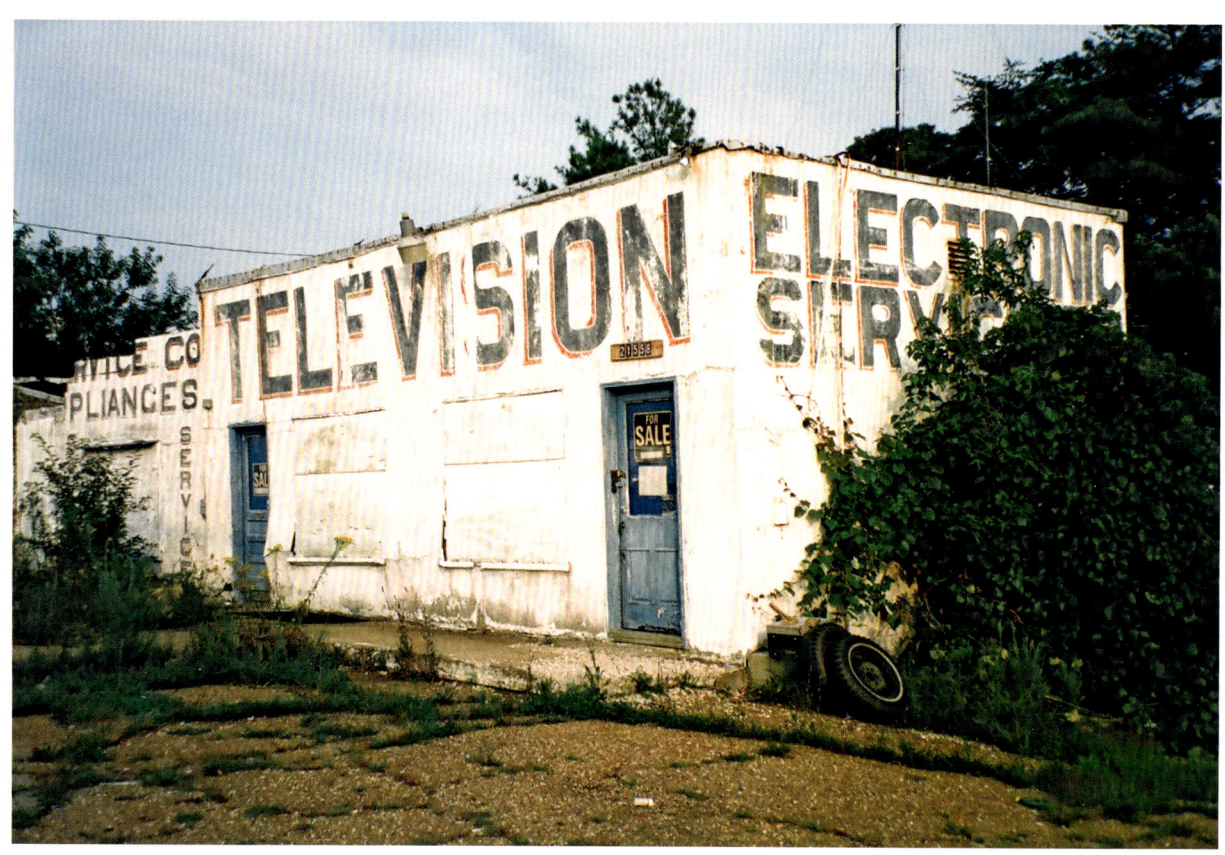

Lexington Park (no longer standing).

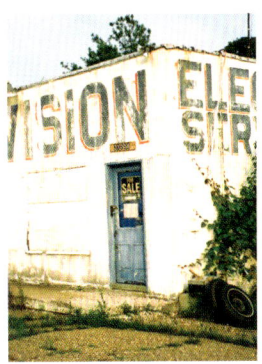

*Now, this here model is the latest thing. It's got a picture clear as a bell,
replaceable tubes, and the screen's the biggest and brightest twelve inches!
Plus, for a little more, you can purchase this magnifying lens, folds down
over the screen, to make the image even bigger.*

MARTIN WAS FASCINATED WITH GADGETS. There were old well-thumbed copies of *Popular Science* and *Popular Mechanics* magazines lying around on the work benches between the half-cannibalized radios and TV sets and discarded sandwich wrappers. He had no doubt dreamed of some-day coming up with an invention of his own. Martin came to work at the shop at twenty-one, just out of war-time service in the Navy. He didn't like to talk much about his experiences in the Pacific, even when his customers would ask. Young as he was, he was soon known as Mr. Fixit and had quite a reputation for being a wizard with tubes and wiring. The first set he owned was a used Motorola Tabletop with a nine-inch screen he got for $50 from a customer who brought it in for repair and then decided to spring for a new DuMont. He practically had to build it from scratch to get it working, but he loved it. When the opportunity opened up to buy the store, Martin was ready.

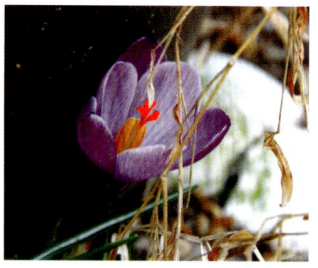

We were so sorry to hear, Agnes. He was a wonderful man,
and we'll all surely miss him.

AGNES THANKED HER FRIENDS for their concern, their casseroles, chicken pies, and crab cakes. The Frigidaire was already full and she had no appetite, but it was thoughtful of them to keep bringing the food over. She told them they were good friends and what good friends they had been to Dan, too, especially those who had visited him in those long final months. The gossip and familiar talk of hog and tobacco prices, boring as it was to her, seemed to comfort him. She thought maybe she'd take some of that good food over to the soup kitchen in Ridge later and share it with folks who could use it. She'd leave the crab cakes for her own dinner, though. She knew her appetite would come back. Just like she knew spring was coming 'round the corner and with it the crocus that would soon be pushing up purple noses to greet her as she stepped out the front door.

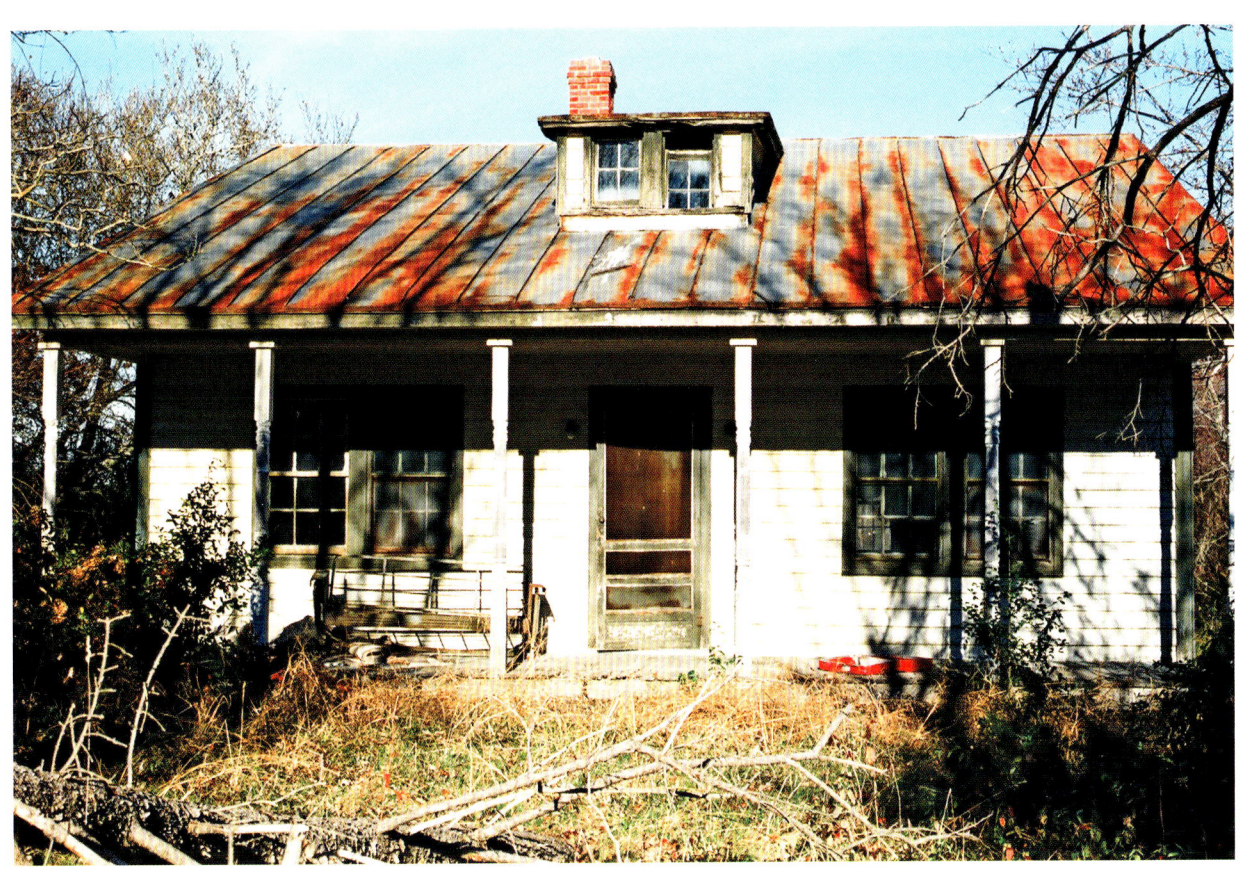

Hilton Ridge (no longer standing).

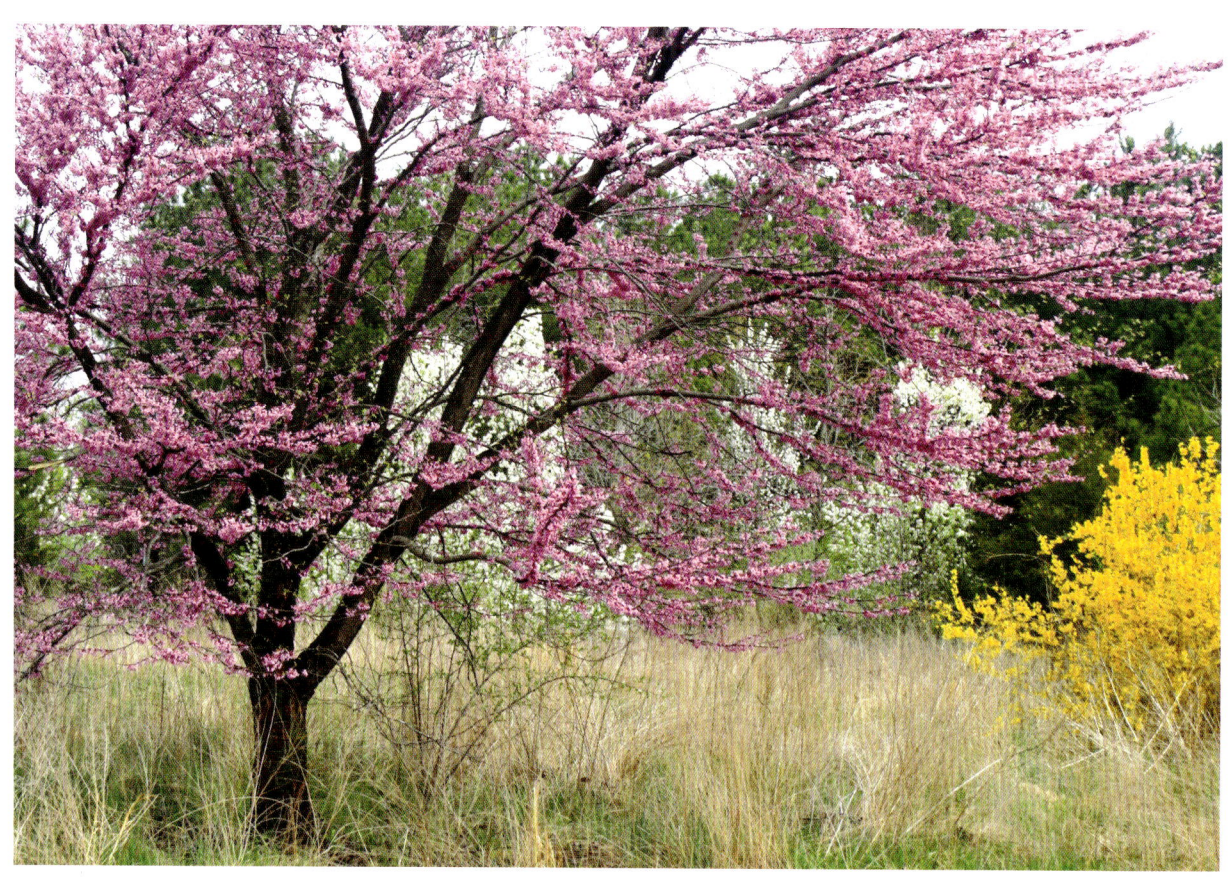

Redbud, forsythia, and wild cherries in a Lexington Park field.

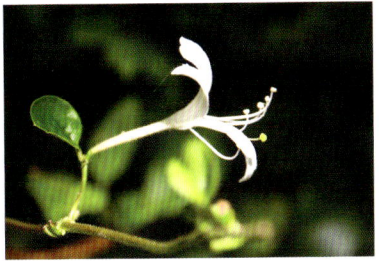

Open the windows, Roy, let some of that cool evening breeze in.
Mmmm, smell that honeysuckle.

ADA DID LOVE THE LATE SPRING, the time between the wet grayness of early spring and the blasting heat of summer. The early spring flowers were always a delight, cheering her with their promise of another growing season. But it was later, when the redbuds and dogwood were in full bloom and the honeysuckle began to release its delicious aroma that she was most happy. She didn't care that other people considered honeysuckle a weed. Nor did she care that the redbud was called the Judas tree by some, because Judas Iscariot hanged himself on one after betraying Christ. You could hardly blame the tree. Ada loved the autumn, too, of course, with its cool nights and stimulating change of colors. She loved those in-between seasons. That was just about the only times you could open your windows and let the outside in.

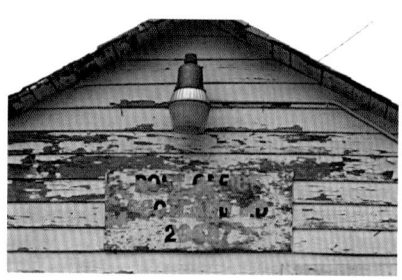

Give me one of those Dr. George Washington
Carver stamps, please, Missus.

"How's that son of yours, Tillie? Couldn't help but notice the letter, putting it in your box yesterday. I knew you'd be glad to hear." The postmaster knew pretty much everything that was going on in that part of the county, sometimes knew more than folks wished she did. Tillie was embarrassed to have her know how long it had been since she'd heard from Bobby. Probably knew, too, just how much Tillie longed to know he was still safe and whole over there in Korea. Tillie decided there was nothing wrong in being friendly. "Well, he couldn't say much, of course, but he's doing OK. Got the socks I sent and wishes I could a sent him some home cookin' along with them. Says it's real cold over there, and the socks are much appreciated." "That's three cents, Tillie. Now, you take care."

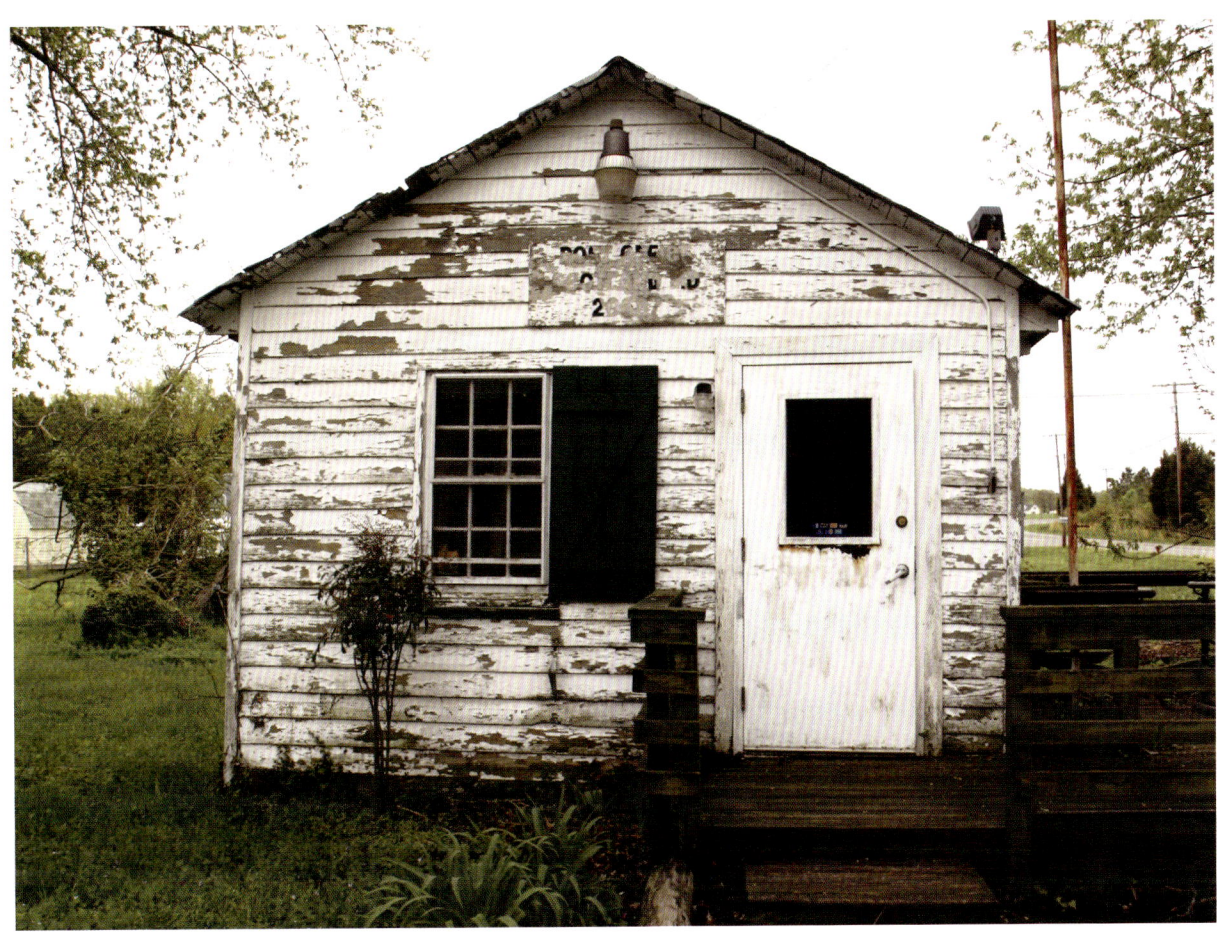

Scotland Post Office (established in 1882).

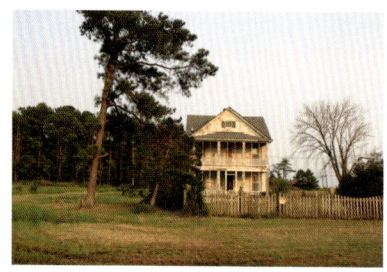

Lila, come down here and help me get this dinner on the table!

Aﬀﬆﬀﬃ ﬔﬃﬀ ﬄﬀﬅﬅﬆﬃﬀﬂﬀ ﬅﬁ '33 came and seemed to blow the family apart along with everything else, life went on. Lila still loved sitting out on the upstairs porch in the afternoons when it wasn't too hot. When she went in, though, the house seemed to have a cool, hollow sound. Like a hollow ringing left in the air after a child's shout or a pot lid dropped and left to lie. It wasn't like that before when they were all together. Maybe there was just too much empty space for their puny spirits to fill without Dad there, she thought. But they had pulled together to clean out and fix up the damage from the big storm. And once Ma started letting out rooms that fall, the house got full and noisy fast. She knew it was a good thing, moving on, but part of her missed that sound, that hollowness he left behind.

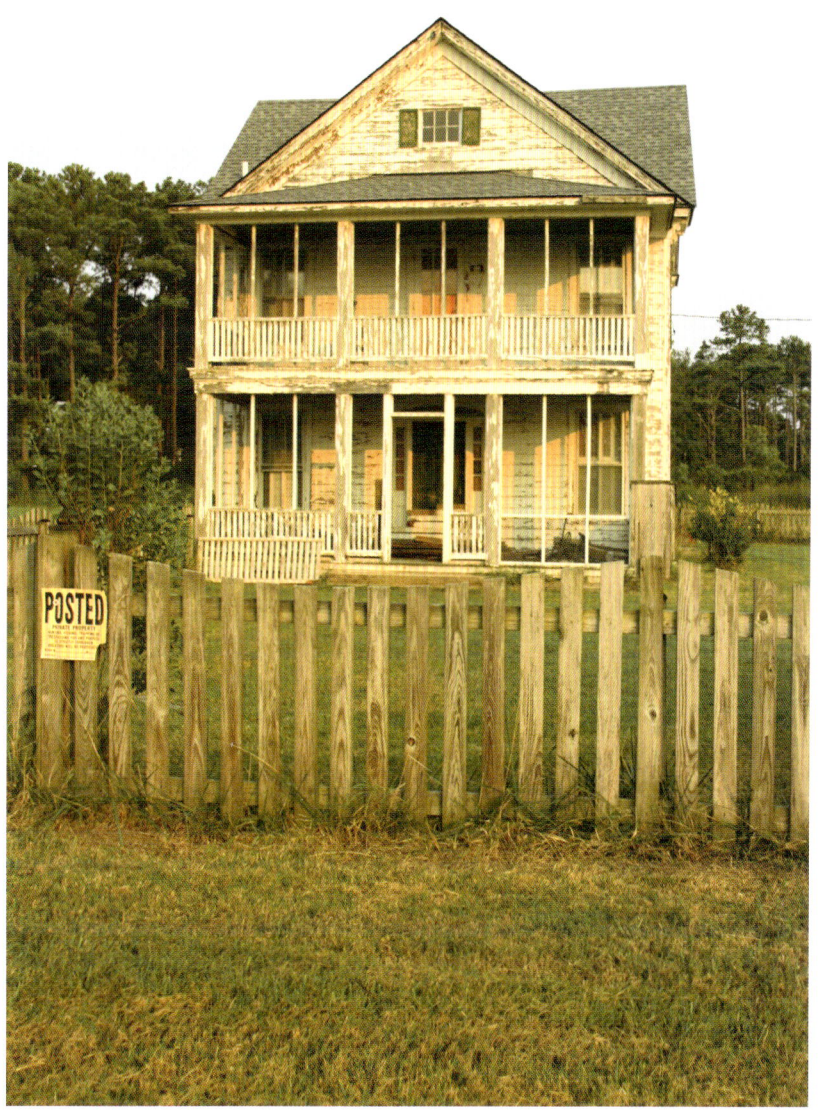

St. George Island.

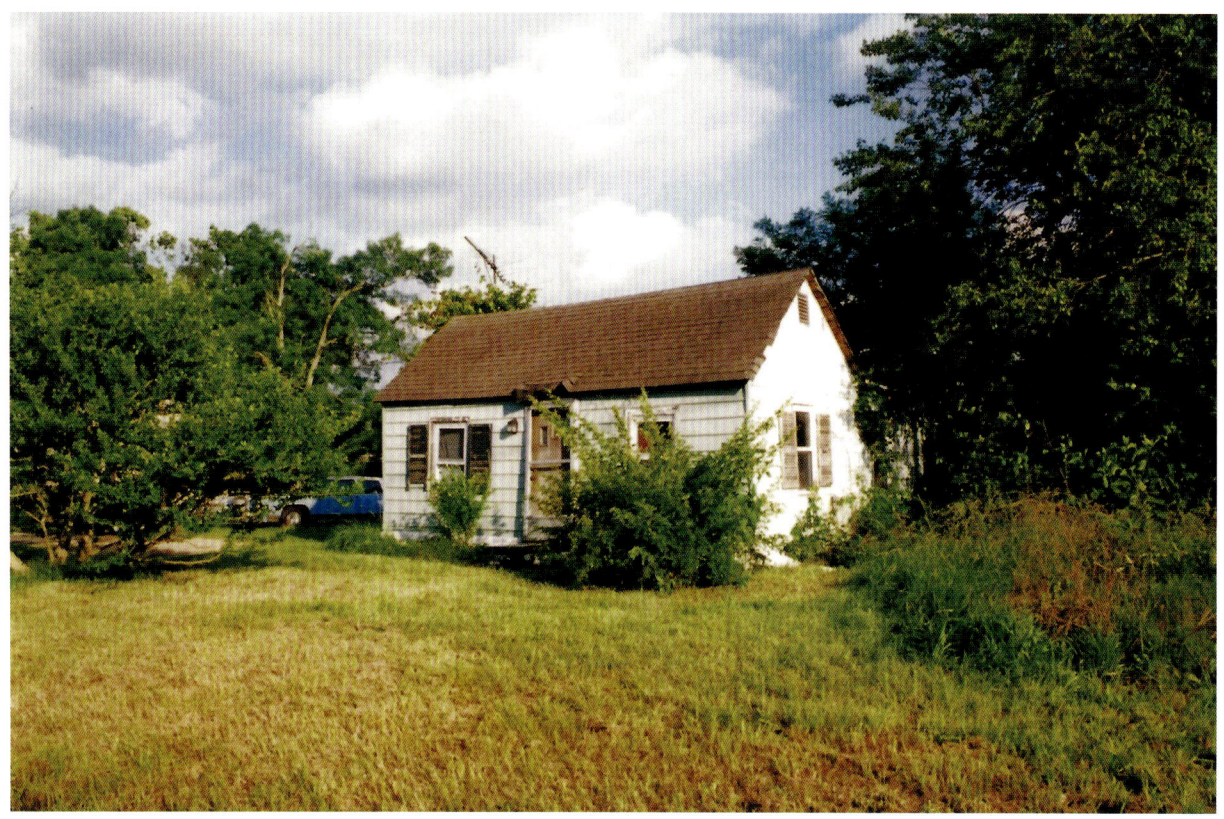

Beachville.

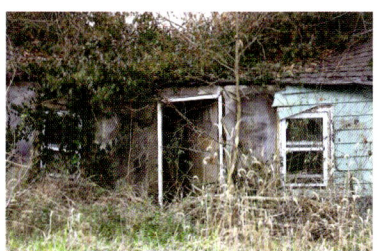

Daddy's home, and he's got big news! Got on a crew at the Navy base. Regular pay check every week! Now, come over here, and give your daddy some sugar.

L IKE EVERYONE ELSE, they had been excited when the Navy base came in and all those new jobs opened up. They thought, "The sky's the limit." Sure, some folks were really bitter, the ones who got pushed off their land. They weren't given much time to find somewhere else to go, and most felt the government didn't pay them what was right for their land. But it had opened up jobs and brought new folks into the county, people who were from all over, bringing in new ideas. The way it turned out, though, seemed like that sky had a low ceiling. Their dad worked hard, but it seemed like he couldn't ever get moved up. Their mom tried for a job on base, too, but she couldn't get anything but a cleaning job. It's different now, and people forget. Their dad had counted himself lucky to get a job with decent pay that wasn't farming or working the water, but it was frustrating seeing the white workers get ahead when he couldn't seem to get to the next level. But the kids still remember that day when he came home and told them he was going to work for the Navy. That was one happy time. They felt like they had struck it rich!

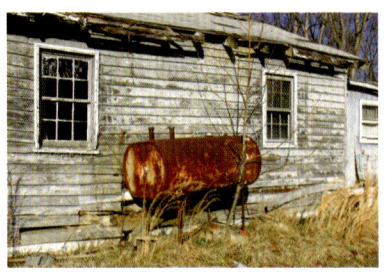

Pssst. Jimmy. Are you awake? Is it time yet?

HER BROTHER, WIDE AWAKE IN THE BUNK ABOVE, whispers back, "Go back to sleep, it's still dark out." But the little girl can't sleep. Not on Christmas morning. They giggle and whisper, imagining what might be waiting under the little tree their dad had cut for them and they'd decorated with popcorn and holly and topped with a tinfoil star. They picture the old-lady stockings hanging by the stove, full of lumps and bumps that make them look like the snakes that had just raided the hen house. They try to be patient. They imagine big smiles on their parent's faces when they open the ornaments they've made for them at school. But they can't wake their mom and dad yet, not even on Christmas. They'll wait just a little longer to put their bare feet down on the cold linoleum floor in the mud porch where they sleep.

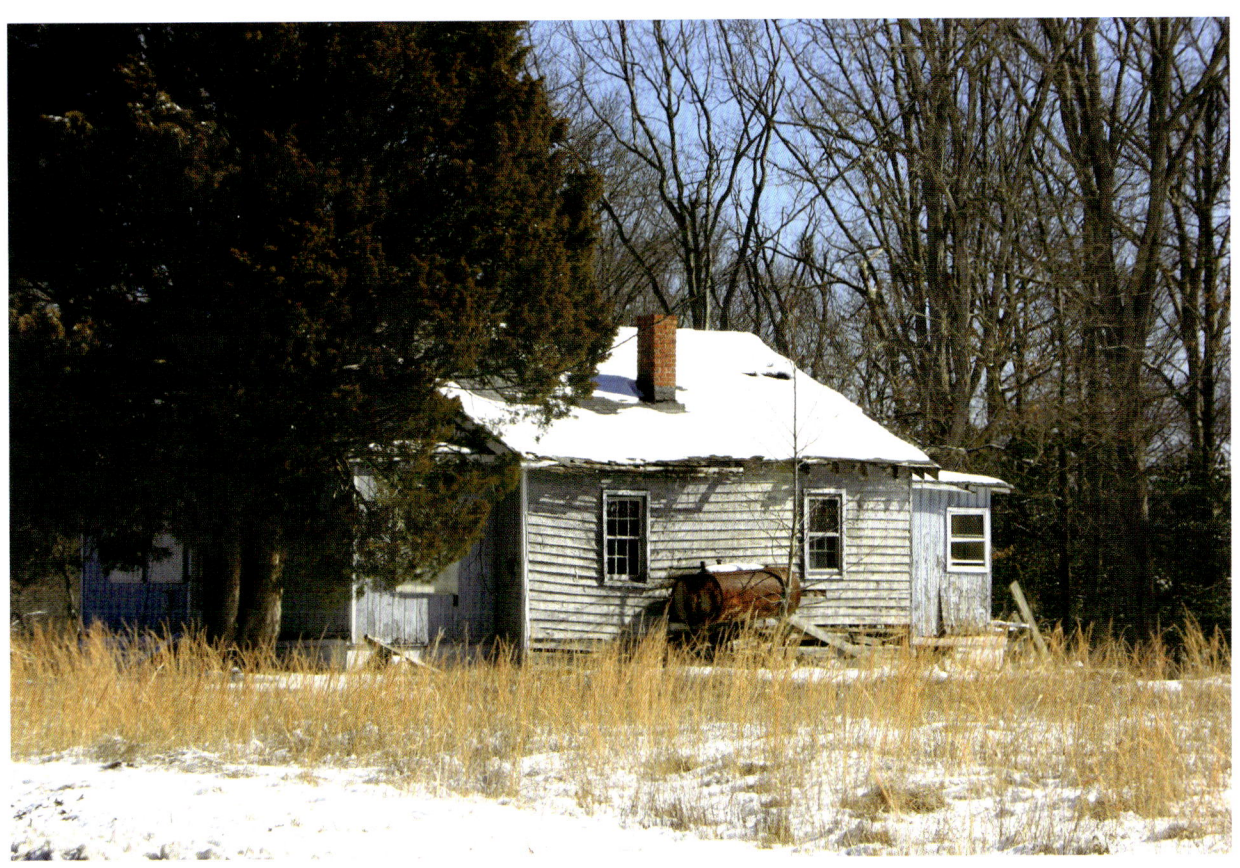

Hermanville Road.

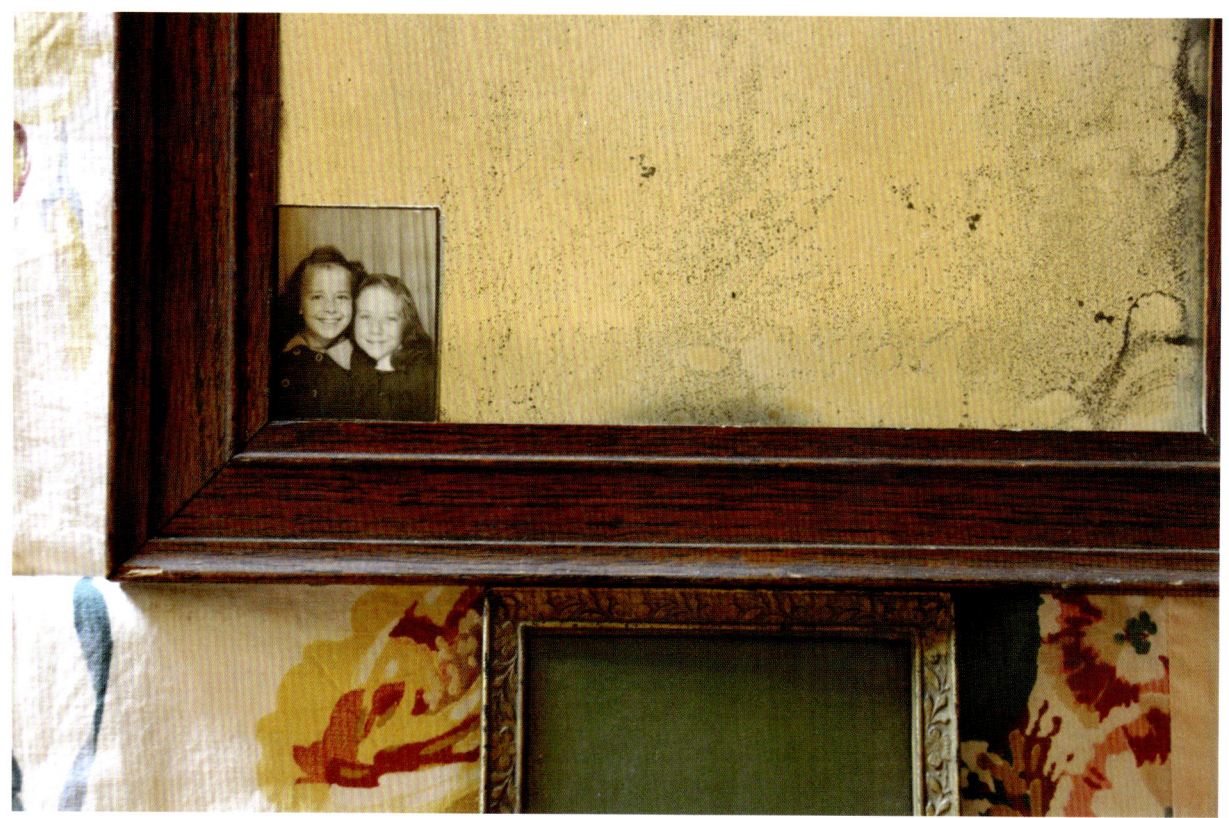

Best friends.

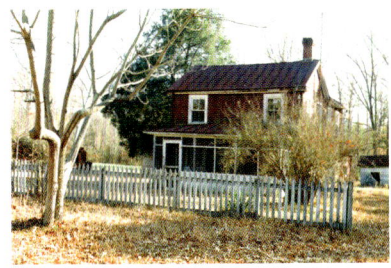

Ouch!

THE TEARS STARTED TO COME as Claire looked in the mirror at the hopeless tangle of hair. Since her mama was in the hospital in Leonardtown, the neighbor lady who used to be a beautician had offered to give her a permanent so she'd look nice for Easter. She had to admit she'd been warned not to try and comb it out herself. "Just come over in the morning, and I'll take out the rollers for you," the lady said. But when Claire got up and started getting ready for the Easter Sunday service, laying out her new skirt and jacket and finding the anklets that went with her new shoes, she didn't want to wait. "I can just do that myself," she thought, yanking out the curlers and starting in with the brush. Poor little girl didn't know you had to unwind those curlers, not pull 'em out any old way. And just jumping in with a brush like that, you could end up with a tangle that might never come out. Her dad insisted on photos from the booth the church had set up, so Mama could see how nice she looked in her outfit. At least her best friend, Jody, was there. That made everything more bearable.

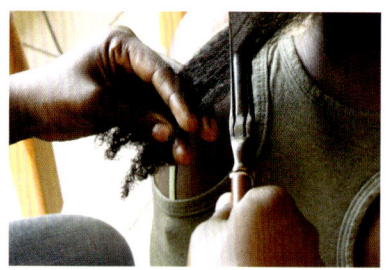

Mama, wake up!

The mother had so many heads to do, she used to fall asleep with the hot straightening comb in her hand. The babies kept coming one after another. Every Saturday night, there were three or four little heads to do, sometimes more. "Girl, go get me the straightening comb," she'd say, and that would start things off. They had a little stove made special for heating the comb. Stored it with the Royal Crown hair grease, curling iron, and the wrappers they called "kids." When Nat King Cole was on the TV, the time would pass quicker. Those girls were always looking sharp come Sunday, every one of 'em. Their mother saw to that.

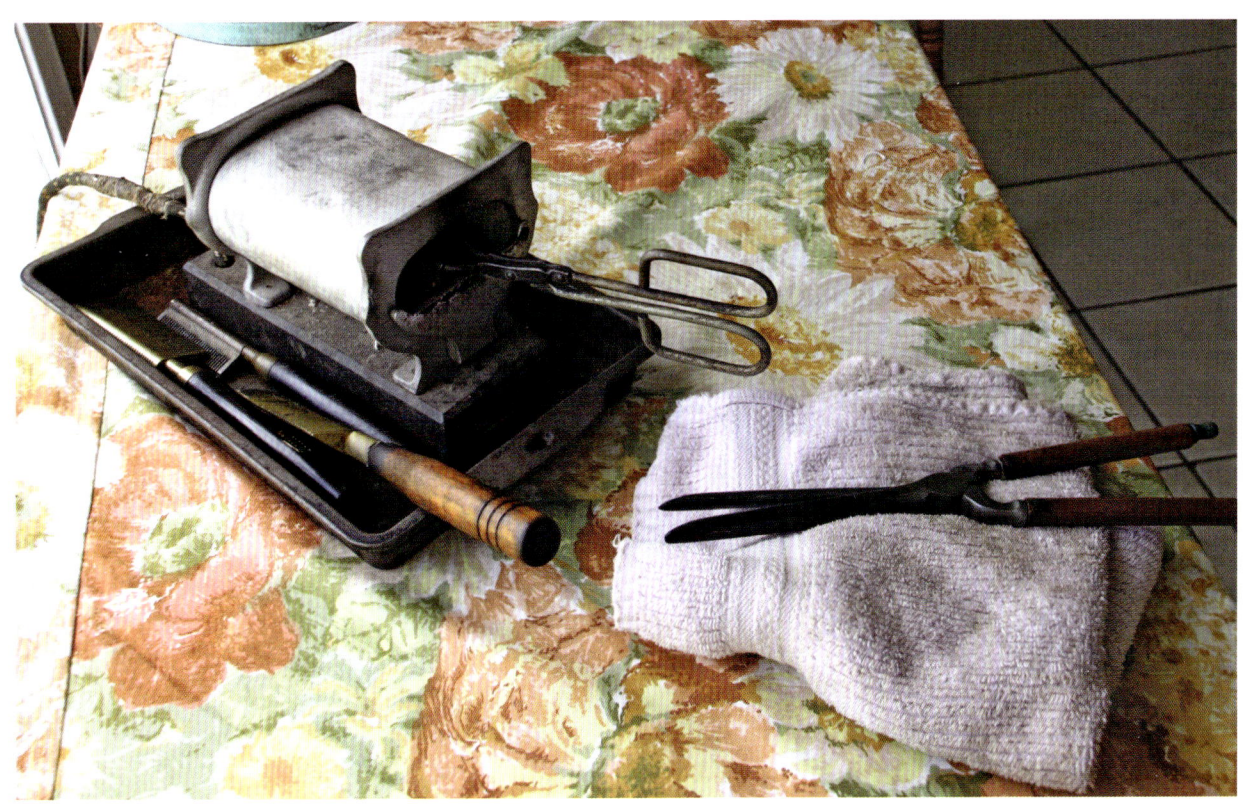

Old-fashioned hair stove, with straightening and curling irons.

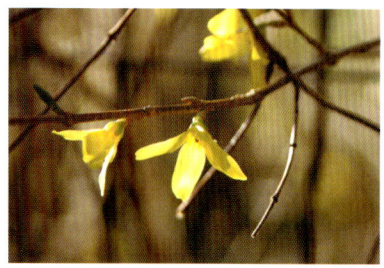

You finished setting the table yet, baby? Why don't you go pick us
a few sprigs of that forsythia out front to pretty it up a little?

The little girl learned that setting the table was a way to practice art. The plates with their roses and lilies of the valley, she loved those. And the silverware, shiny stainless steel. "So much more practical," her mama said. "This is how you arrange it, just so. Get everything spaced out and lined up even." At dinner, all the plates matched, and they didn't use the plastic ones like at lunch. When company came, they had cloth napkins. The girl learned how to iron on those napkins. Then, the best part was the flowers. She had two favorite vases, a little clear glass one with wavy edges her granny gave them and one in the shape of a duck. Maybe it was supposed to be a pitcher for cream, she didn't know, but they used it for flowers. Her mama always let her pick the flowers. They had jonquils and grape hyacinths out back and yellow forsythia by the front door. She'd just cut a little bit of that for the table, so folks could still see each other. That was important, not to make the bouquet too tall. Her mama taught her how to do things right.

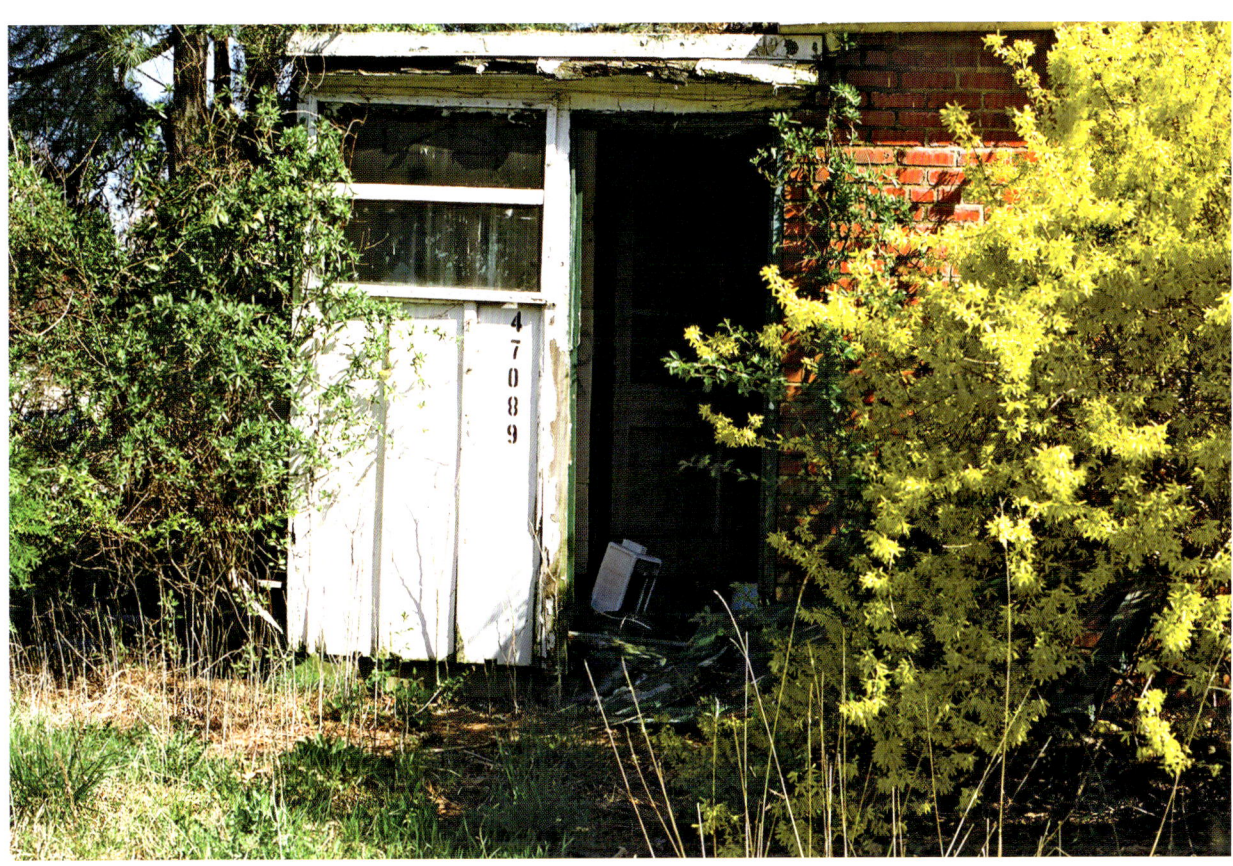

Lexington Park (no longer standing).

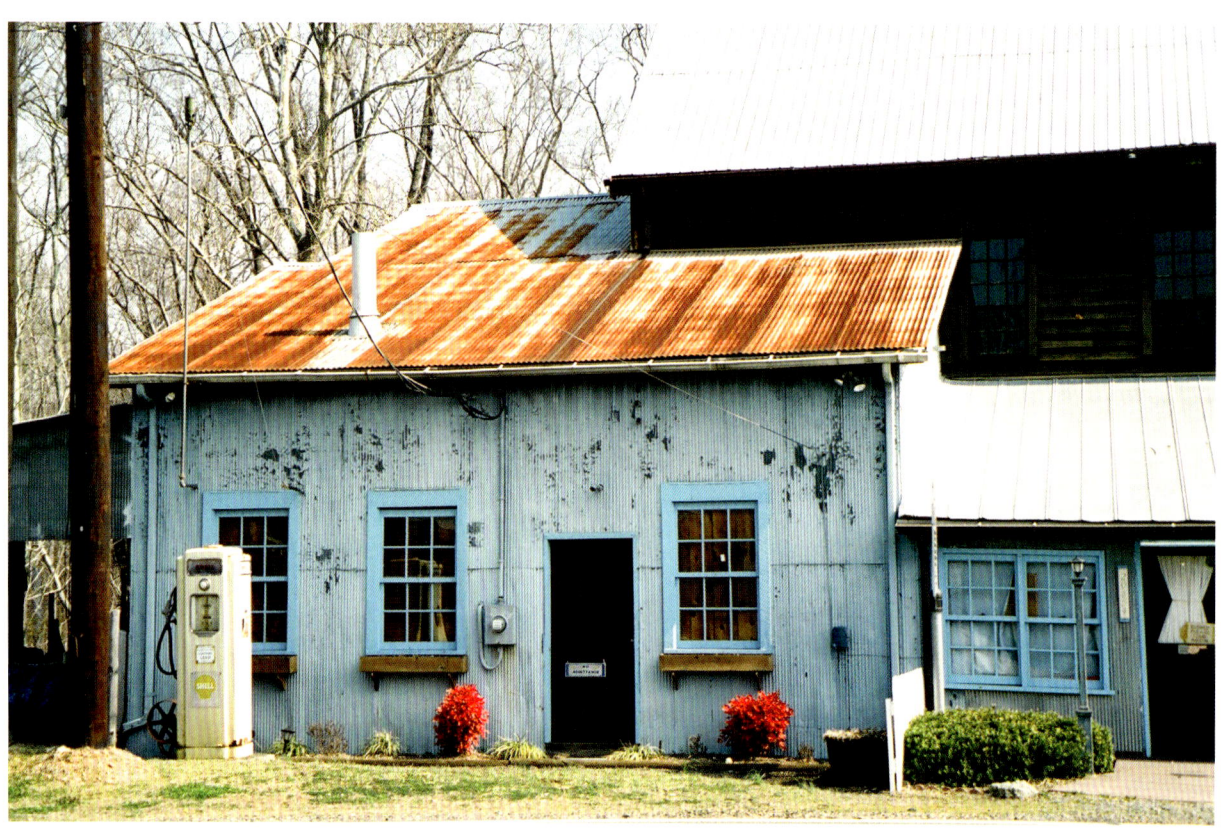

Cecil's Mill on Indian Bridge Road.

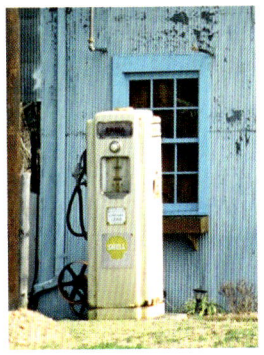

Wooee! Thirty cents a gallon! Gas prices get any higher,
we're gonna be sittin' here on our butts goin' nowhere.

FRANK SMILED and tipped the attendant anyway, even as he shook his head. He rolled up the window and put his new DeSoto in gear. In a funny kind of way, being able to complain about it but still be able to afford it put him in a good mood. He was on his way up, he thought, as he pulled out and joined the flow of traffic. He flipped on the radio and sang along with The Drifters, "Money, honey, if you want to get along with me." Now, that was a top hit he could really relate to.

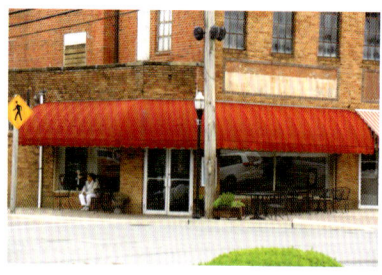

You turn around and walk right on out of here, Auntie.
That bus going to be along soon. You go on and just
wait for it out there.

S HE HAD HOPED AGAINST HOPE that she could wait inside the drugstore for the bus up to Washington. She knew not to expect to be served at the lunch counter, but it was cold and windy out, and she had on just the thin coat. She could see a few men standing back in the arcade by the stairs up to the movie theater, where she knew she wouldn't be welcome either. She'd heard they served booze back there. She pulled her coat a little tighter and stepped out the door. There were no signs posted in the store or restaurant window, but everyone around here understood. They knew who was welcome and who was not. The sit-ins and protest down south hadn't made much of a ripple around here, at least not yet.

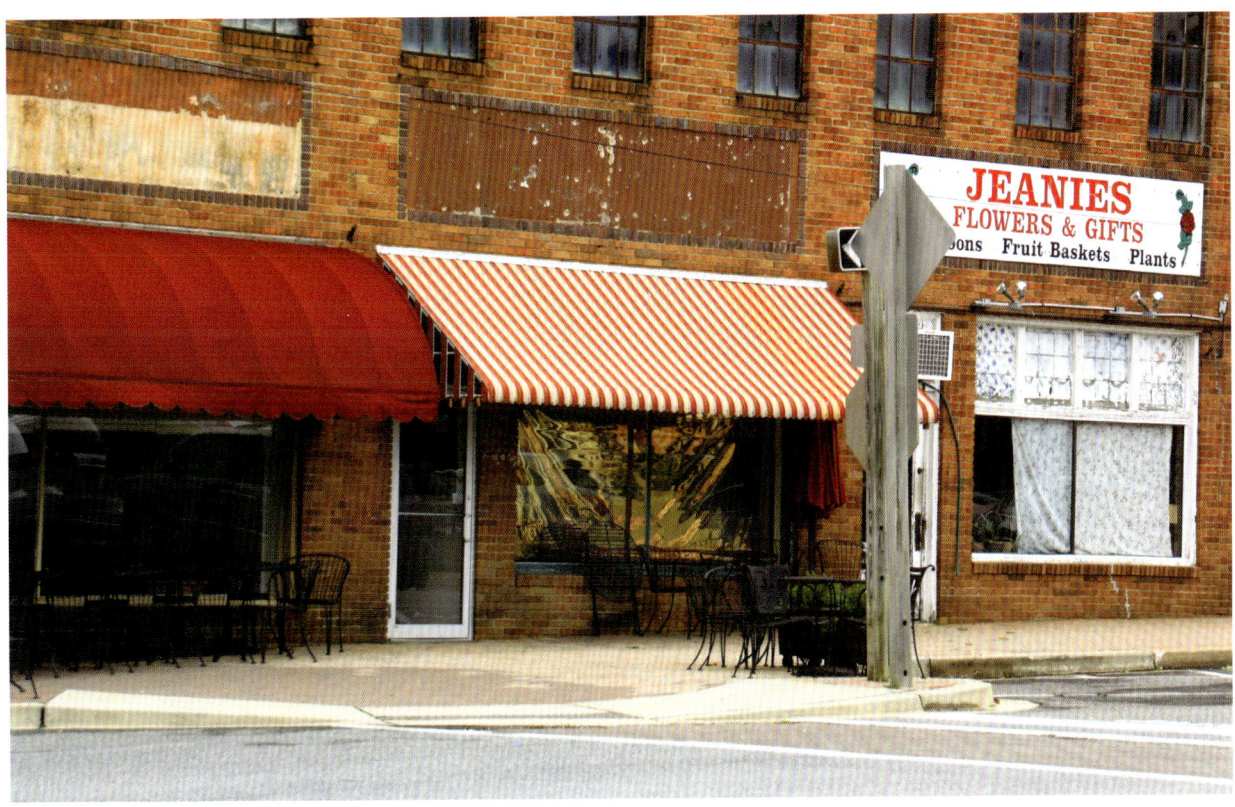

Leonardtown Square.

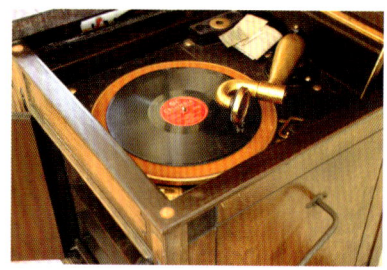

"You can roll it, you can "slop it," and can stroll it at the hop . . . "

ESSIE HIKED UP HER SKIRT an inch above her knees, put her hands on her hips, and started swiveling her feet. Little brother Bobby laughed at her, taking on the challenge, and stuck his hands down in his pockets, making his hips and feet do all the work. The kids loved to put the records on the old Victrola and move out on the porch on warm evenings, when they could leave the door and windows wide open. They'd do the "Slop," the "Mess Around," you name it. Sometimes, brother Harry brought out his guitar, and they'd get into some serious boogie-woogie. And if the wind was right and the sound carried as far as the neighbors, those kids'd be in the yard, too, doing all manner of flinging and swinging each other around or just falling down, laughing at each other. Essie sure wished her mama was still around. She would 'a been outshining 'em all.

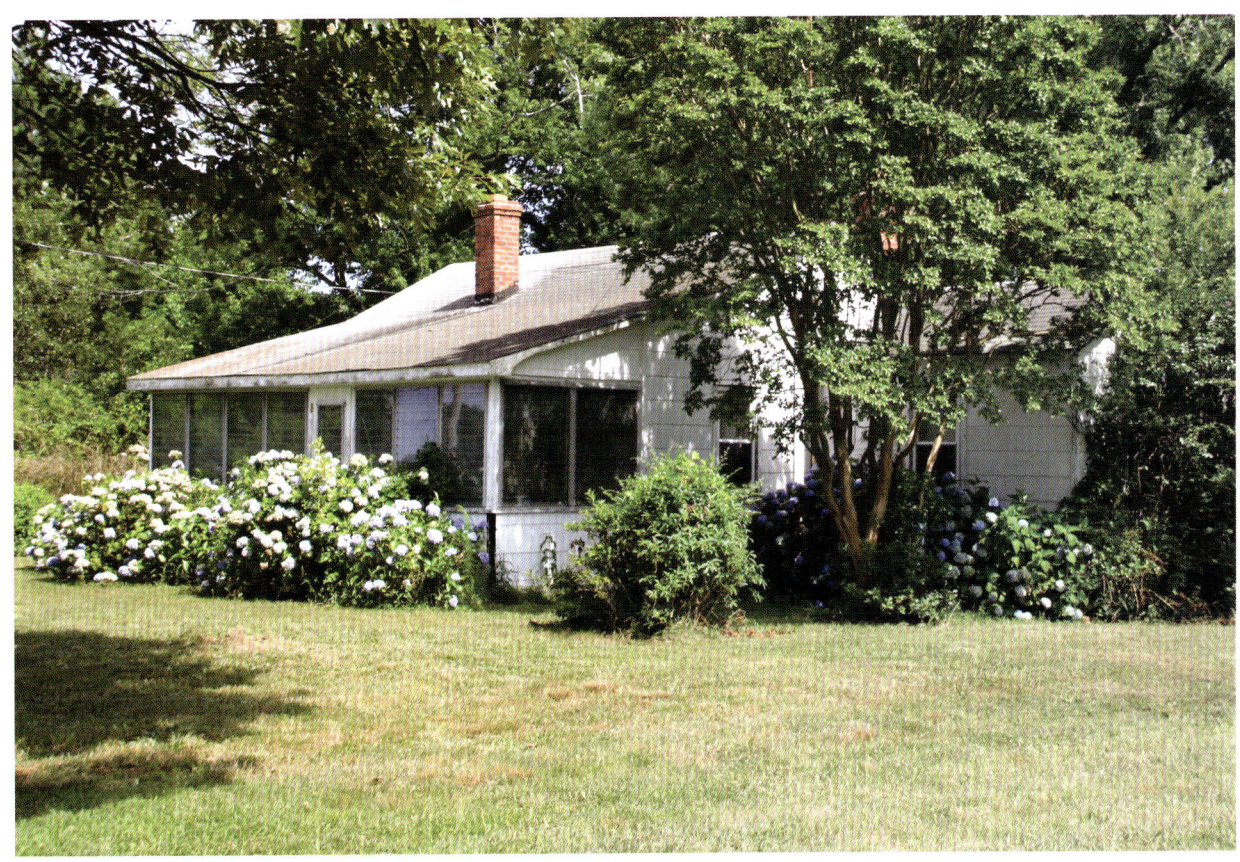

Wynne Road in Ridge.

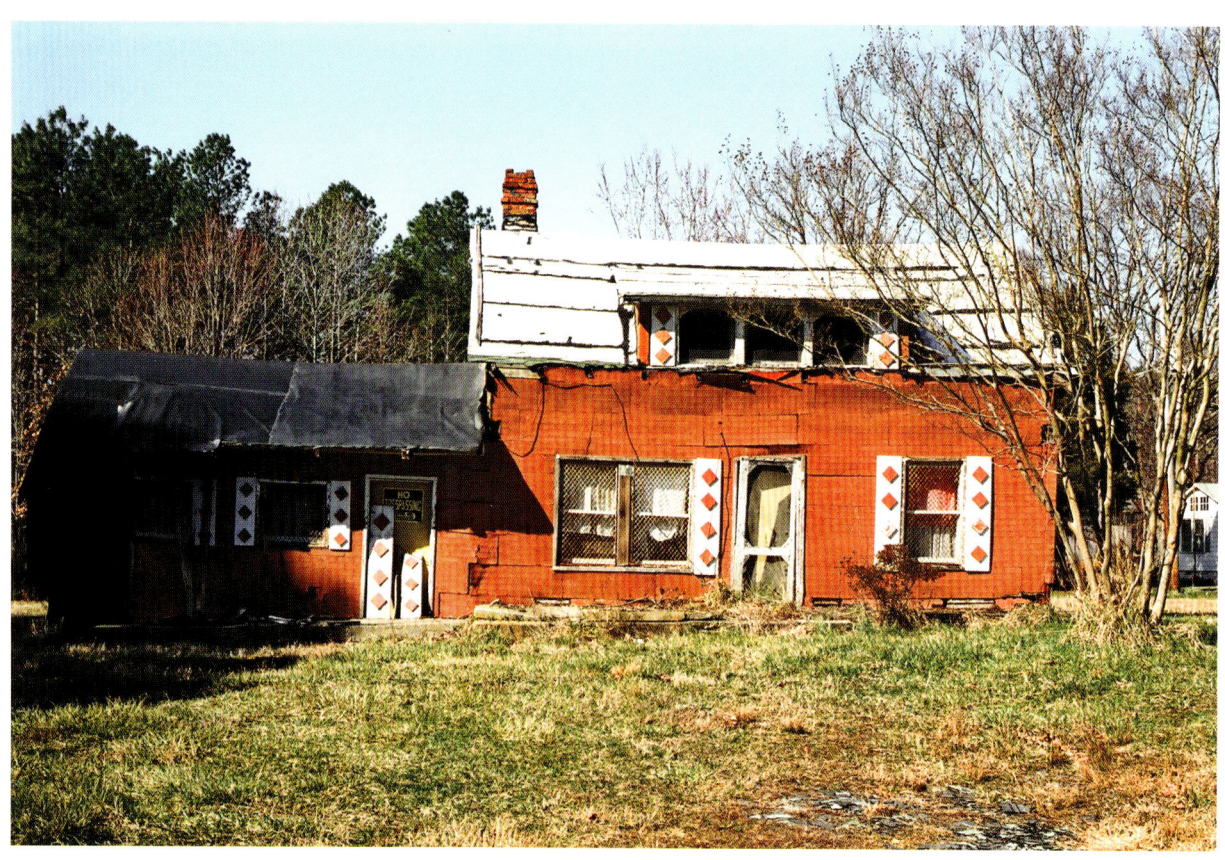

Ridge area (no longer standing).

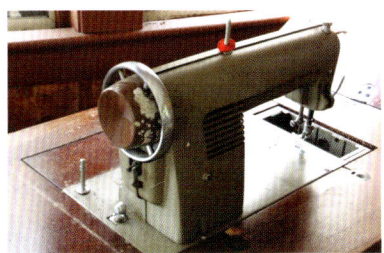

Come over here, Sister, and try this on. I need to mark the hem.

SISTER WAS ALWAYS BEGGING HER MOM, "Can't I have some store-bought clothes for a change?" Sister's friend, Ebony, had gotten the prettiest outfit for Easter, and it came all the way from a store in Washington, D.C. Sister's mom was a really good seamstress and made extra money doing mending, hemming, and making dresses for other folks. Her mom would always ask, "Why you want that ugly old thing anyway? I can make you something twice as pretty. Come on, you can help me pick out the fabric." Sister secretly thought it was because her mom couldn't bring herself to buy clothes from a store that wouldn't let folks like them in the dressing rooms. The stores down here didn't have signs or anything, but everyone knew who was allowed and who wasn't. Sister's folks never made a fuss about things like that. They just stayed away from trouble and tried to make a nice life for the family. They worked hard and were always fixing up things around the house. When Sister was sixteen and working a job after school, she walked in that store and picked out the prettiest blouse they had, walked right past the clerk into the dressing room, and tried it on. She gave it to her mom for Christmas. That year, her mom gave Sister a nice, almost brand-new Kenmore sewing machine.

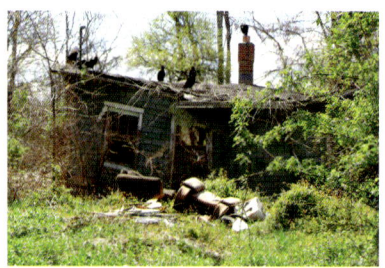

You kids get up from that TV and go play outside!
Summer'll be gone before you know it.

THE CHILDREN'S MOTHER was always trying to get them to go outside, get out of her hair. The boy and his sisters would be glued to that TV, watching "Sky King," "Broken Arrow," and the one they loved most, "I Love Lucy." They'd be laughing their little kid laughs, and their mother would be yelling from the bedroom, "Go on outside. Watching that TV gonna wreck your eyes!" She was pretty much bedridden those years, hardly got up 'til their father came home. But she'd manage to make them something for supper and sit for a bit before she went back to bed. Sometime, she'd watch Ed Sullivan or Sid Caesar with them. Their dad liked those shows. Their parents wouldn't let them watch "Amos and Andy," but they'd watch it anyway when they could. They thought it was funny. Their mother would get up during the day when the children weren't home and watch her soaps, at least in the early days. She died when the boy was thirteen and the twins were nine. She yelled at them, because she loved them and wanted them to go outside and enjoy being children running around healthy. But those summers were hot, and they loved that TV. They didn't get one 'til long after their friends had one. Maybe, they felt they had to catch up on what they had missed.

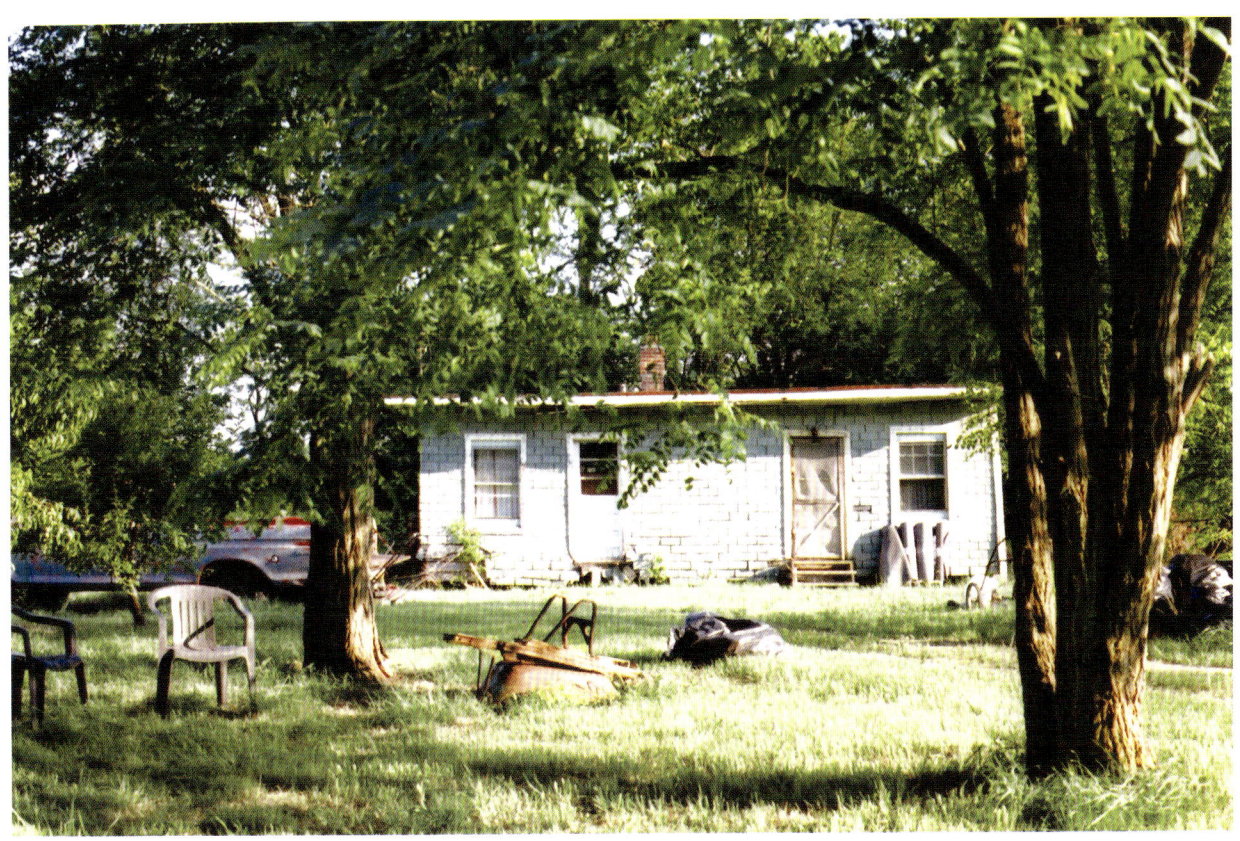

Beachville (no longer standing).

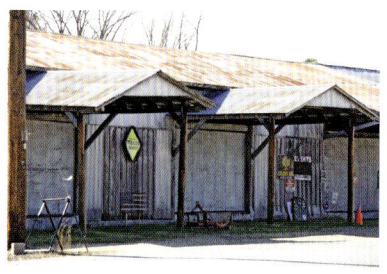

Who'll give me forty-one, forty-one, forty-one, forty, done.

THE AUCTIONEER WAS QUICK TO SEE the eyebrow twitches, hand taps, and fist pumps that signaled bids. The auctioneer's rhythmic chant and fast-paced exchanges with buyers excited Buddy, and the trip to the tobacco warehouses was something he looked forward to all year. With the endless hours of stripping leaves, hanging, and packing finally behind them, he and his dad were happy to breath in the sweet smell of the tobacco, "the smell of money," his dad said every time. Buddy knew his dad worried about the prices and how they jumped up and down and whether he'd make enough to cover expenses and all that. But Buddy just enjoyed the scene and the time with his dad away from the fields and the work. Tobacco was how his family had made a living forever, and Buddy figured it was his future, too, but his mama was pushing him to go on and get more schooling, to get out of the fields. One thing he knew for sure—he didn't want to wear a monkey suit and sit inside all day.

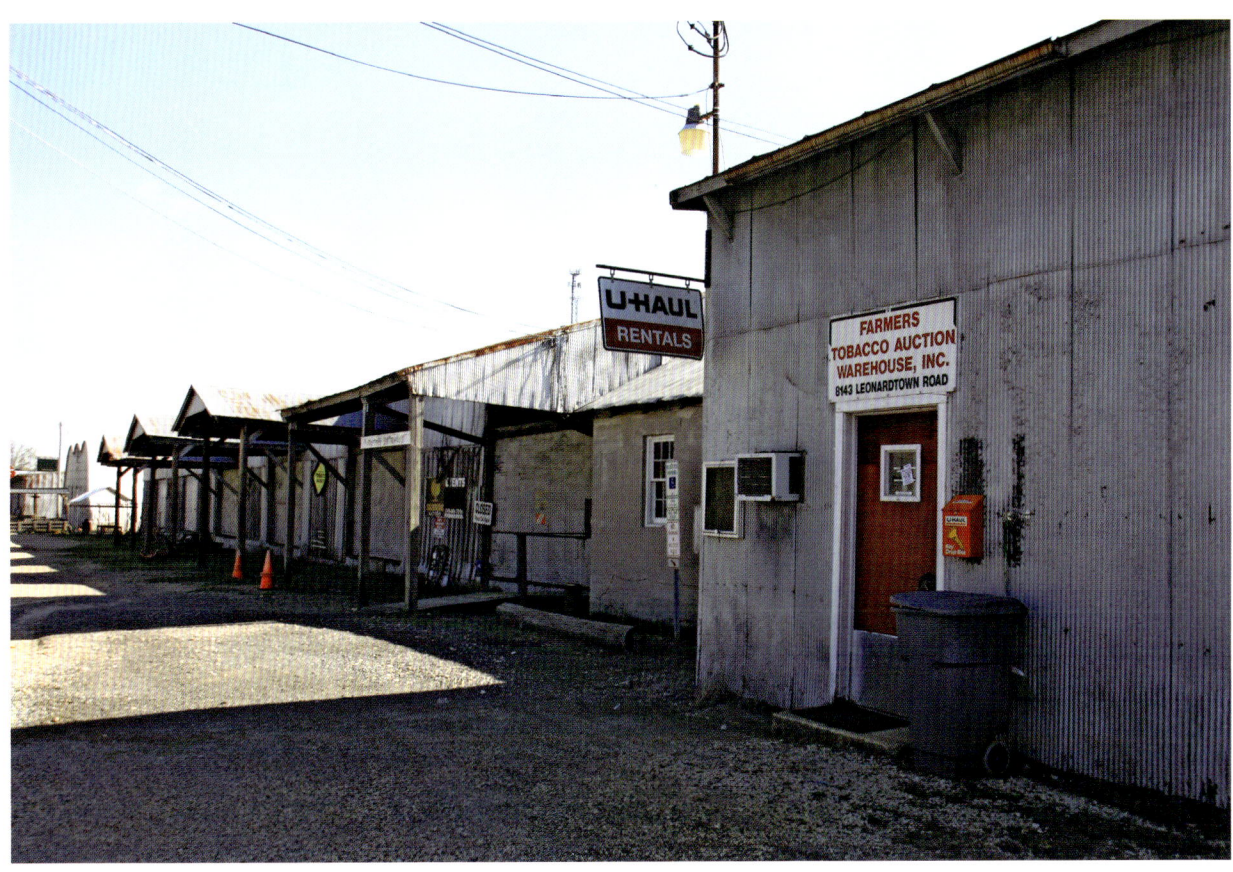

Tobacco warehouses in Hughesville.

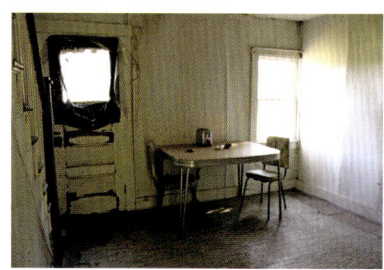

Quit your jawin,' woman, and give me a break! You think
I'm not trying? A man needs a drink and some friendly talk
from time to time. Now, leave me be.

T IMMY USED TO TRY AND SHUT HIS EARS by stuffing them with cotton. His mom and dad fought all the time, all the time. They didn't care whether Timmy or his little sister, Shelly, was there or not. It bothered Shelly more, but she'd stay right there and listen. Timmy just tried to shut his ears and go someplace far away in his head. The yelling would always be the same. She'd be begging the dad to stay home, do this, do that. She'd be crying, and he'd end up getting madder and madder and finally storm out cussing them all. He drank a lot those days. One day he just left and didn't come back. Their mom moped about the house a long time 'til she finally went out and got a job. Things got better for them after that. But she was lonely and took up with another guy, a friend of their dad's, and it wasn't long 'til the fights started up again. She was looking for something she just wasn't going to find with the men she knew. Maybe, it wasn't to be found.

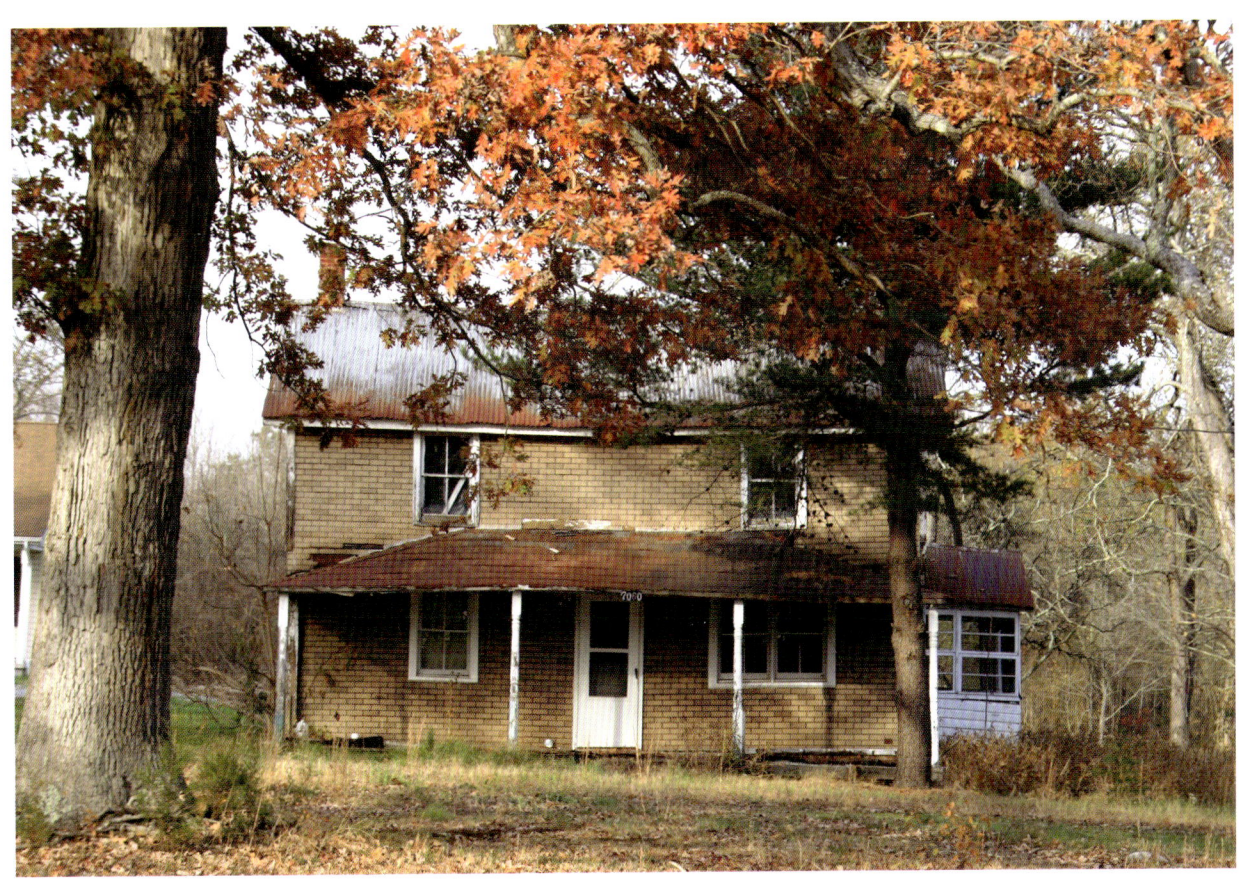

Near the Charles County line.

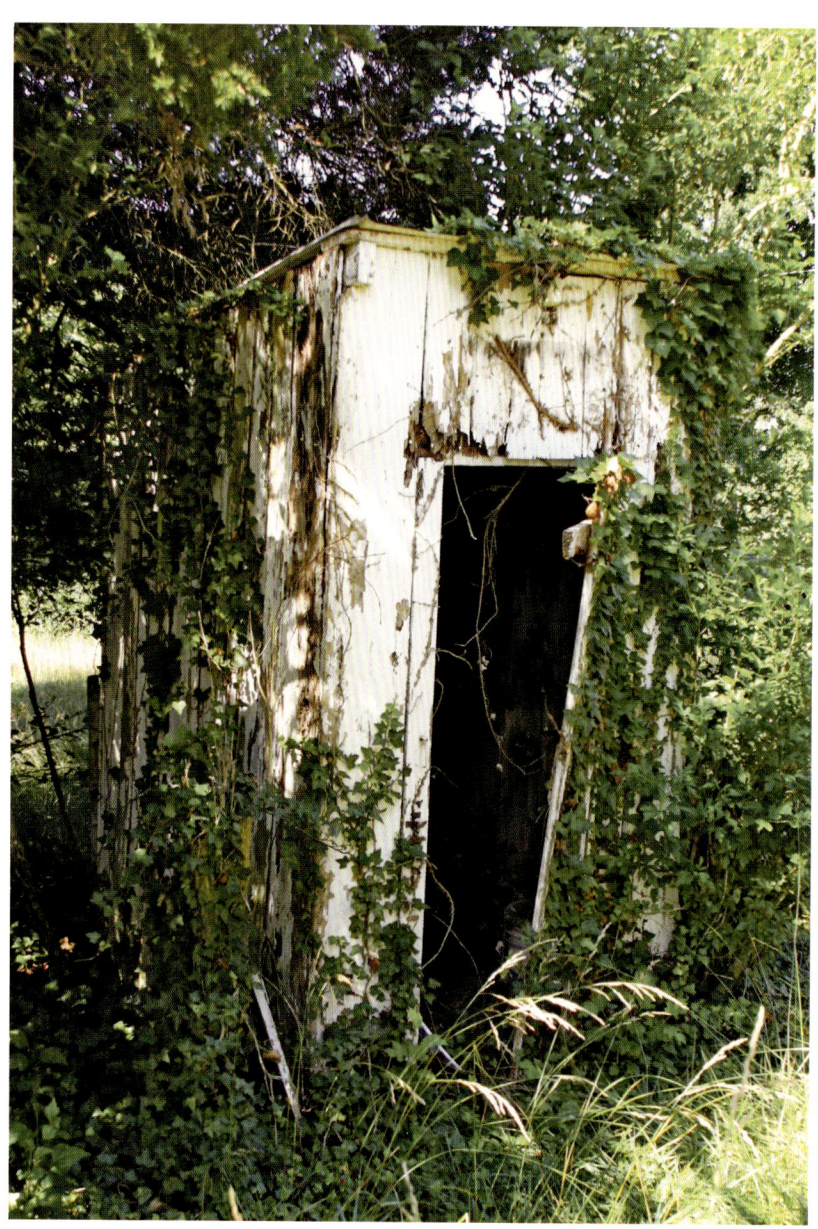

A one-holer (single-seat outhouse).

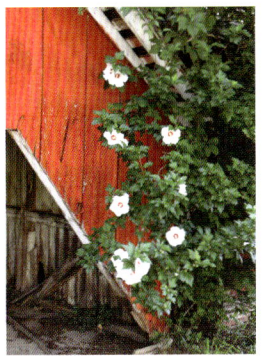

Scat!

JENNY SHOOED AWAY A FLY. She always left the door open a crack to let in the light and air. It's not like there was anyone around who'd care anyway. She could just see the rose of Sharon climbing up the chicken-house wall, and that got her started on making a mental list of seeds to order for her fall kitchen garden. She really didn't mind sitting there when the weather was like this. Planning her gardens was a favorite pastime, and she kept copies of Burpee's and Gurney's catalogs in the outhouse. She loved looking at the pictures and reading about all the new varieties. Most of the time, though, she just dreamed it up in her head. There were always limitless possibilities to consider 'til she got right down to writing a check and mailing off that order.

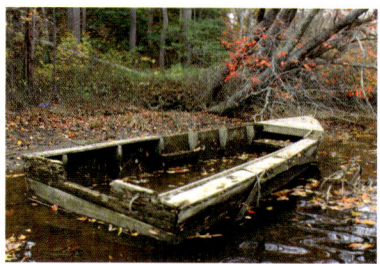

I'm glad the sun's not shining this morning.
A perfect day for crabbing is still and not too hot.

STANDING IN THE FORE OF THE SKIFF, Millie flipped and dipped the net, demonstrating for her passenger just how to rake in a running crab. "When you catch your own seafood, you appreciate it a little bit more," she'd told her. She told her, too, how the crabs would reverse fast or know enough to wiggle and stir up the mud when something was after them. How they knew enough to protect themselves that way. Millie'd been crabbing since she was a baby, strapped on her mama's back. Her mama would wade through the lush eel grass that grew then all along the shore. Those grasses were mostly gone now and the crabs gone with them. When she was coming along, she and her brother used to go where there was grass out 500 feet, and you could see bottom. You could get all the crabs you wanted, and the kids sold 'em for forty-five cents a dozen, not bad money in the thirties. Crabbin' wasn't real work then. And she still didn't think of it as work. It was good to get out there where it's peaceful and quiet and watch the birds and things.

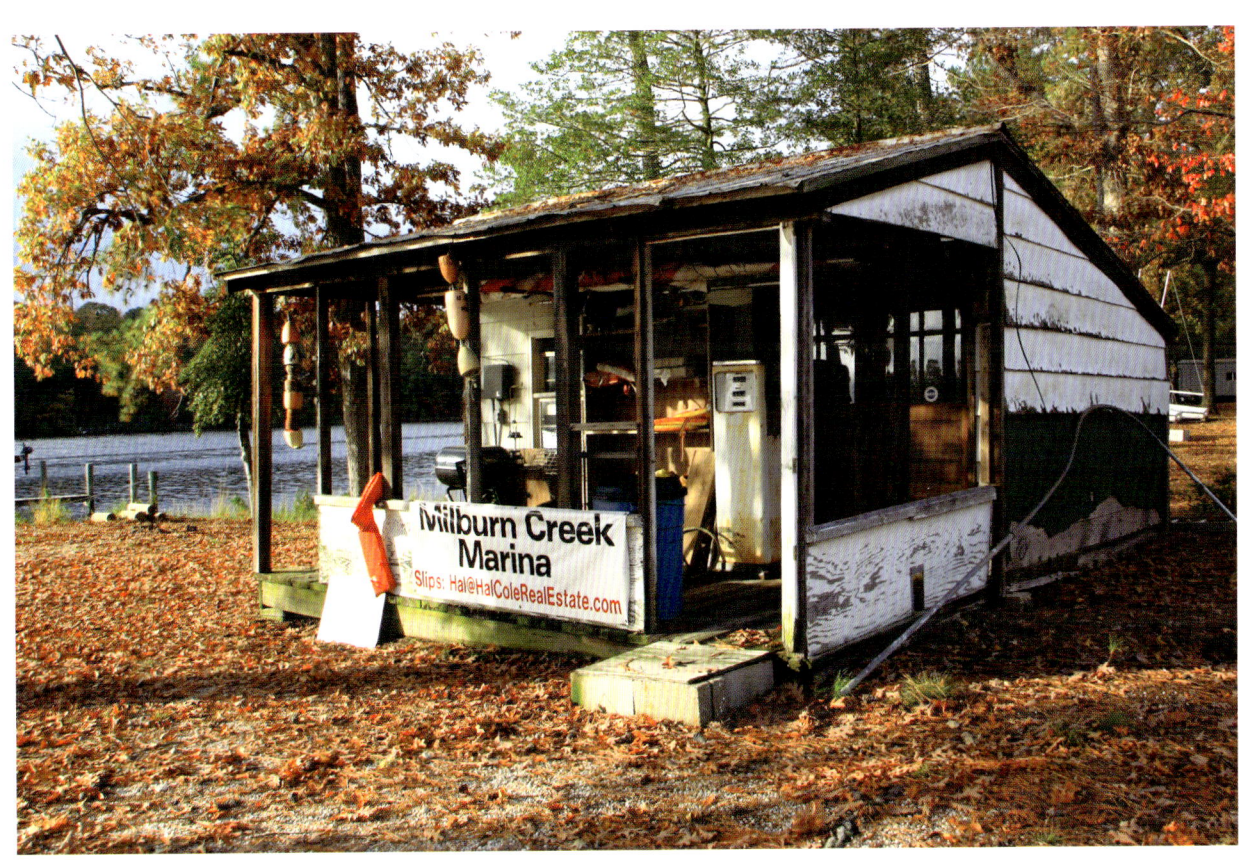

Milburn Creek Marina near St. Mary's City.

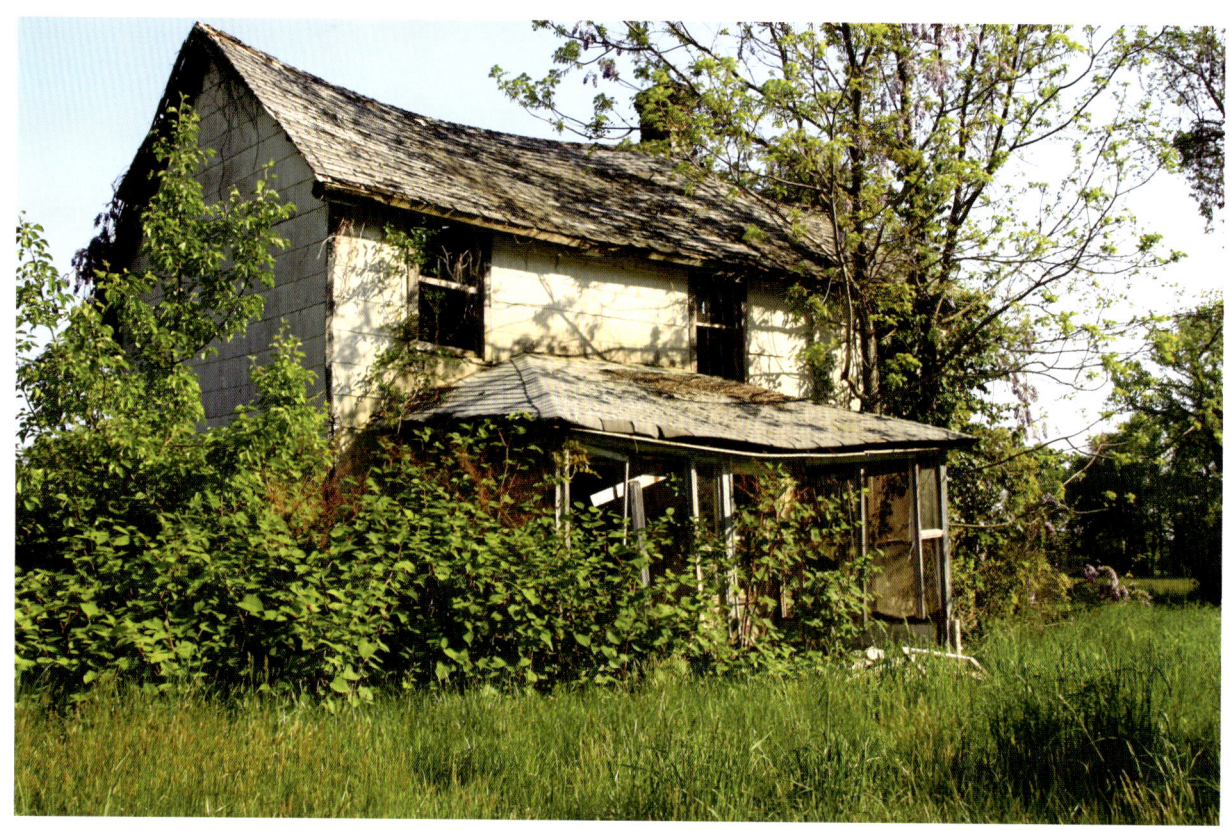

Beachville Road.

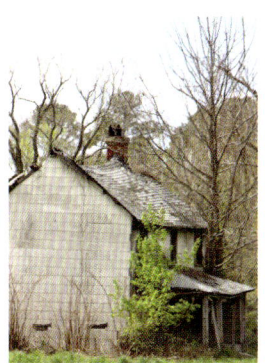

Cal? Give my hand a squeeze, hon, so I know you're hearin' me.

S HE LOOKED AT HER HUSBAND LYING THERE and let her mind drift back over the years. All in all, they'd made a good life of it. She was sure he'd agree with her, though they never talked like that, in a summing-up kind of way. Calvin had a gift for making the land productive, and she could always find ways to bring in extra money. She was clever. And they spent wisely. Yes, that was something else they'd agree on. It hadn't been one of those great romances, the kind she read about and dreamed about when she was young. Not hardly. They'd been heartbroken when the children they'd hoped for didn't come along, but they'd managed to get through it. The thing was, as different as they were, they fit together somehow in a way that worked. And it had worked for a long time. She just wished now it'd been a little longer.

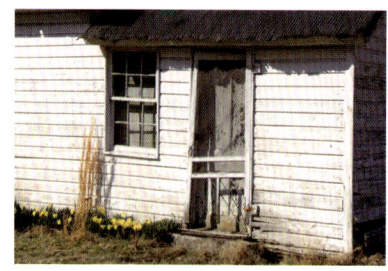

Come over here, all of you, and meet your baby sister.

MARTHA'S MOM HAD A BABY EVERY TWO YEARS like clockwork. Martha was the oldest. Her mom finally stopped with Jesse, the youngest, when Martha was eighteen. Needless to say, Martha spent her childhood changing diapers, running after kids, and playing "mom." She loved those babies, but she thought maybe it was too much of a good thing. That house was always growing but never fast enough. You couldn't find a corner to get any homework done, even if you could get enough quiet, which you couldn't. She knew her mom was following what she thought was right by the church, and she and her dad seemed happy enough. The big family all got along for the most part. But it seemed like there wasn't a time when they weren't worried about getting food on the table and scraping up the money to send all the kids to school at St. James. Martha thought she'd do things a little different when the time came for her to settle down.

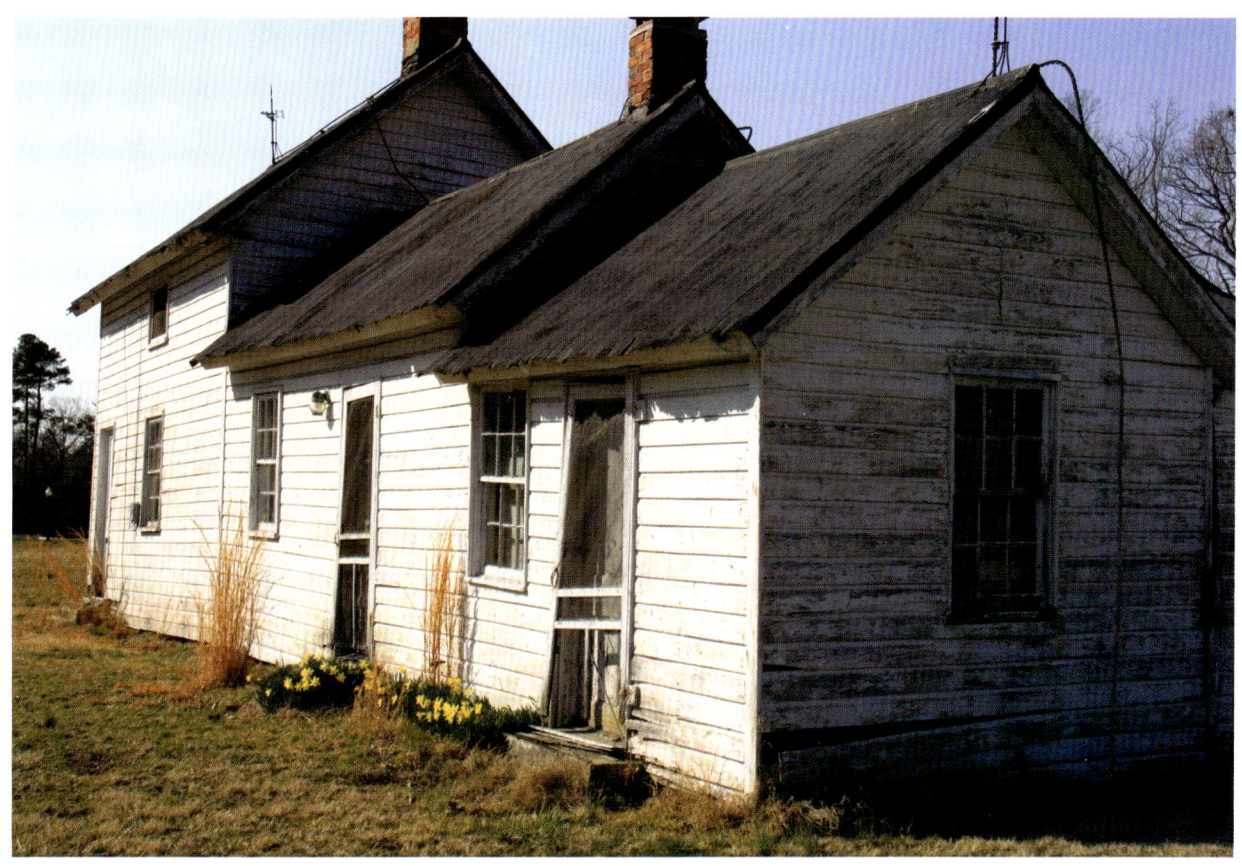

Bull Road.

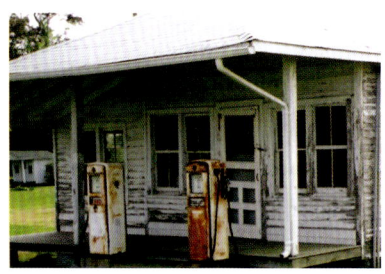

Fill 'er up with regular, and check those tires would you, Harry?
I think that front right one might be a tad low. Got to drive
a long way today with a heavy load.

"SURE THING," MR. MURCHISON. Harry thought Mr. Murchison was one of the nicest guys he'd ever known. It's a shame what happened. Some folks just can't let others be, even if it has nothing to do with them. And one thing they can't stand is someone coming down here and trying to change things. Mr. Murchison made 'em feel like he thought he knew better about how things should go around here. Always making suggestions about this and that at the town council meetings. The real trouble started when Willie Tyrone Johnson got it in his mind to enroll his kids in the white high school in Pamonkey. Mr. Murchison thought that was just fine and got to pushing the town to go ahead and integrate all the schools. Started talking, too, about the difference in teacher's salaries and how it wasn't fair. He even goes and gets a lawyer down from Washington and gets them involved. That caused a hornets' nest like you wouldn't believe, and folks who didn't even have kids got fired up. Well, Mr. Murchison had a business servicing vending machines in the stores around the county. When all that stuff went down, owners of those stores just went and cancelled his contract. Zip. He didn't have much choice after that. No one was going to do business with him. Packed up his wife and kids and headed out. Sometimes, folks have bigger ideas than they can handle or other folks are ready for.

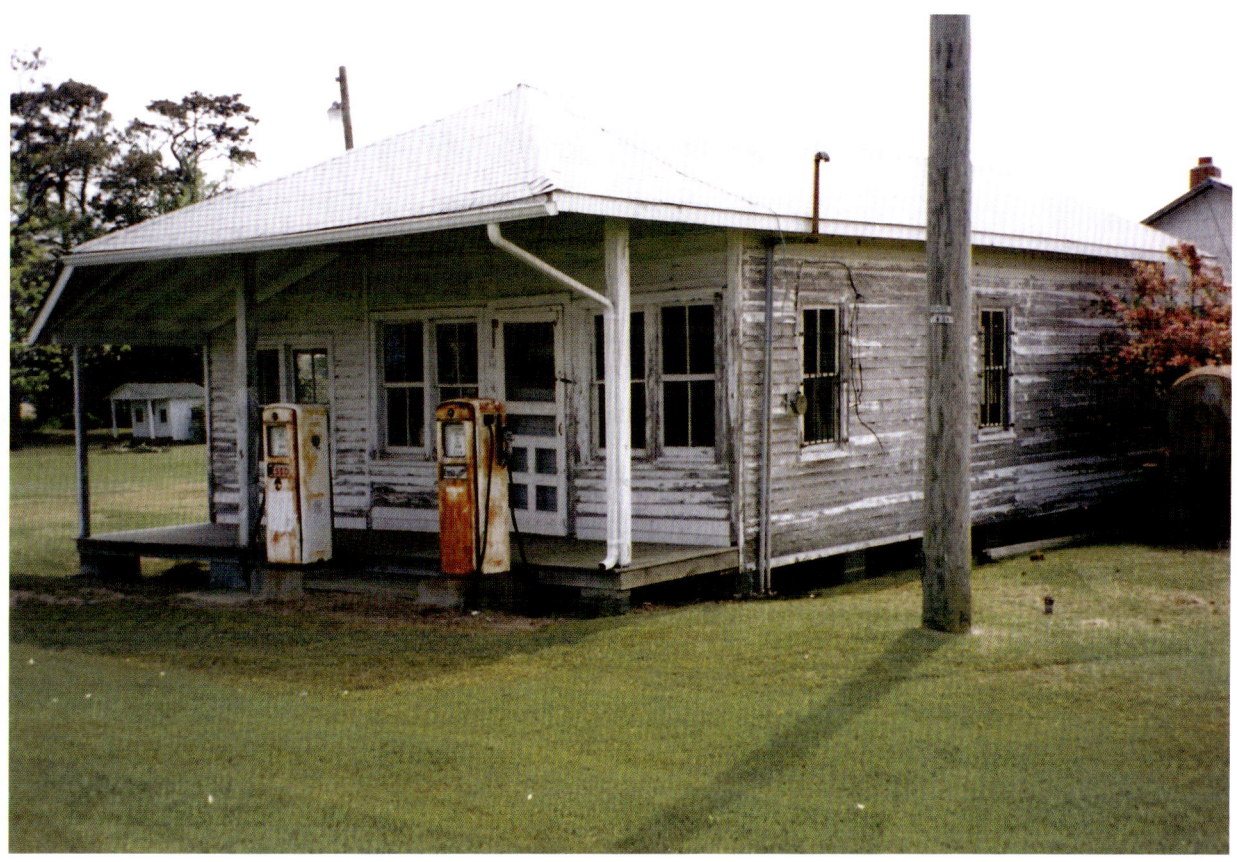

Backwoods gas station and store.

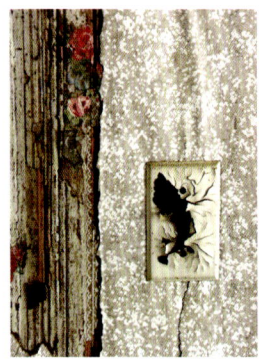

Mary Lou? Is that you? It's almost midnight, young lady.
Where have you been? Your father and I have been worried sick!

THAT DARN SQUEAKY FLOORBOARD had betrayed Mary Lou, just as it had her older brother, Delbert, in his teen years and, long before that, Uncle Nathaniel, who had been notorious for his carousing before he got civilized by marrying Aunt Gertrude. No matter how light and sneaky-footed they tried to be, there was always that one board gave off a squeak that could be heard in the back bedroom. Her mother, wrapping her robe around her as she came into the kitchen, flipped on the light switch, squinting in the sudden glare. Up close to Mary Lou, sniffing for any telltale odors and looking hard into her face, the lecture went much as usual, ending with the usual dire predictions and punctuated with the usual final threat: Her father would see to her in the morning! Mary Lou was of the opinion that the offending floor board had been placed there just so parents could keep their young under lock and key.

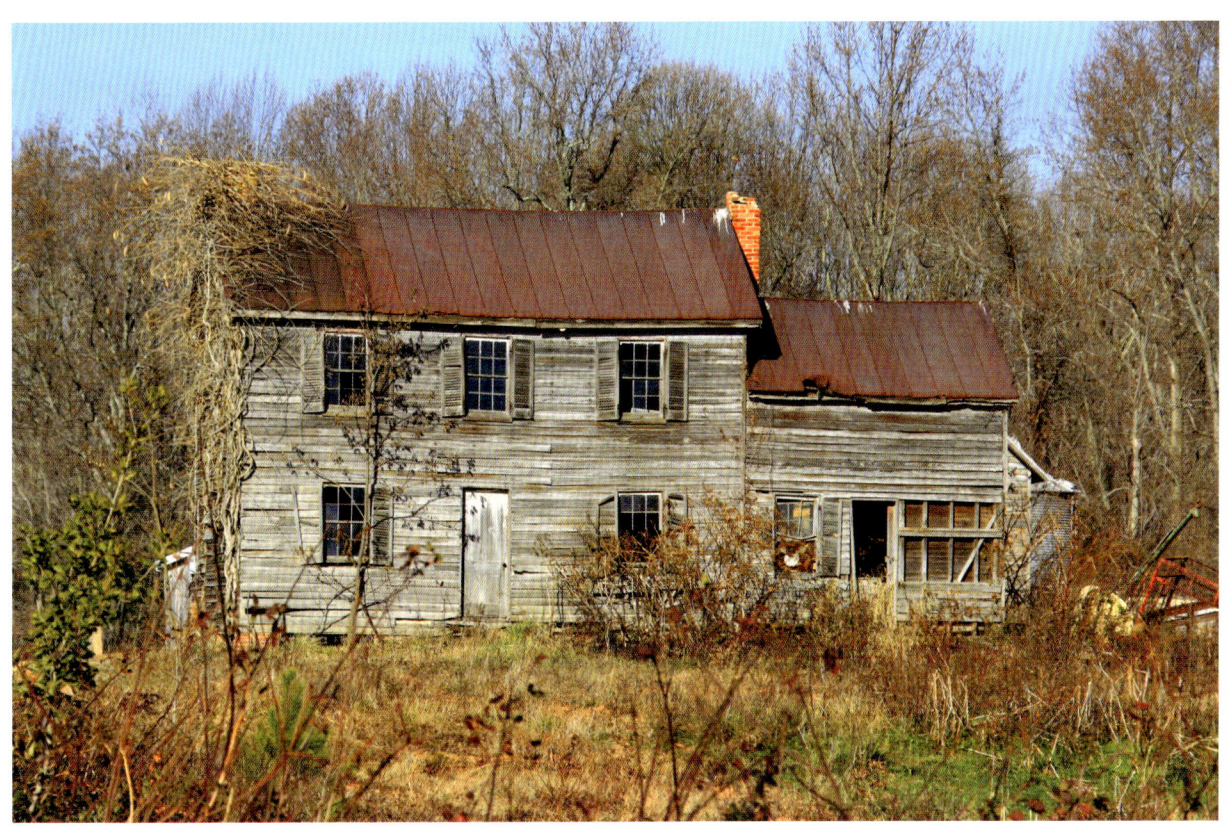

McIntosh Road.

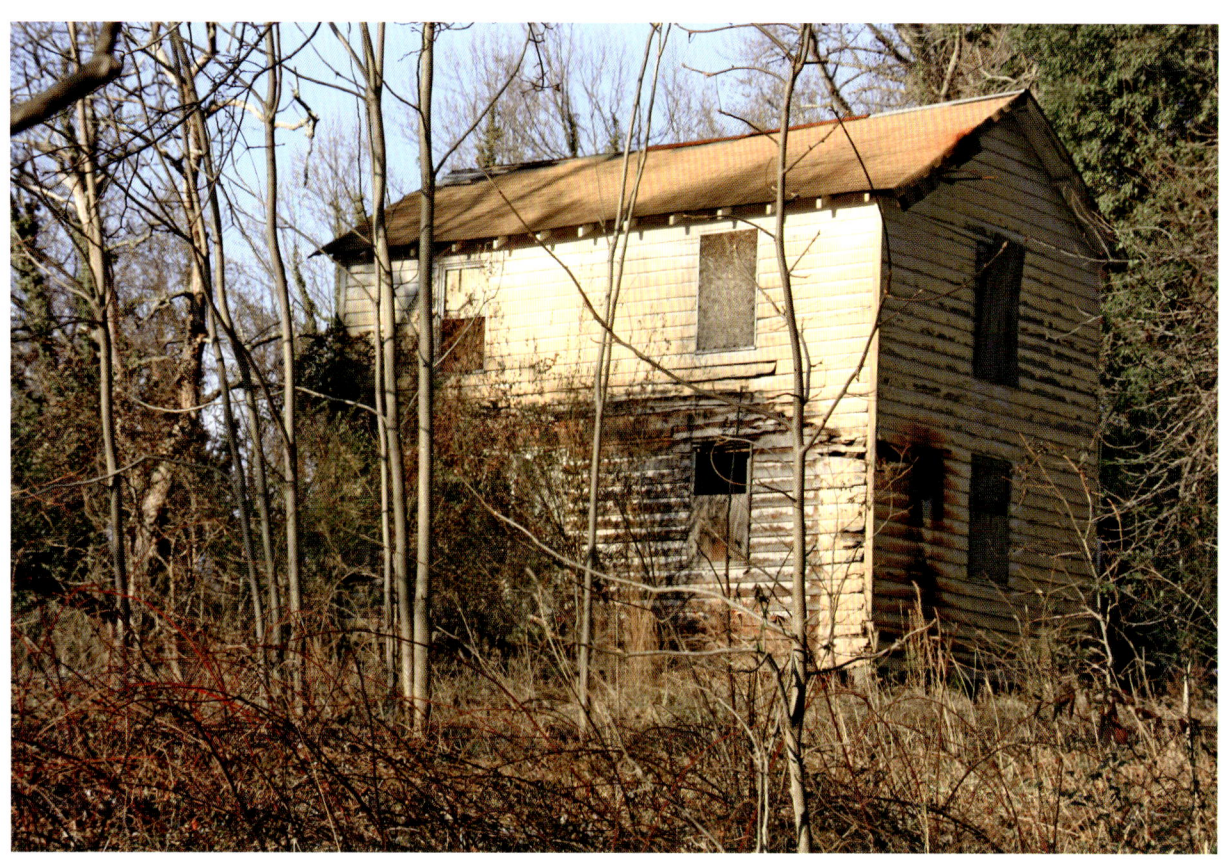

Point Lookout Road.

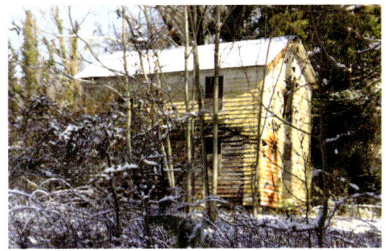

Forgive me, Mom, Dad. I'm truly sorry to cause you the pain.

Putting down the pen, he turned to look out the window and watched the snow falling on the side yard for a moment, not seeing the robin that had taken cover under the forsythia hedge. It was past understanding. The woman who had long hoped to marry him said, "He did it out of anger." At the repast, they milled about the living room, sampling the casseroles, voices muted, sending sideways glances of equal parts pity and keen curiosity at the family who remained stone-faced and dry eyed. If it was anger, who did he mean to punish by it? Or was he already so tired of life, young as he was, that he just didn't feel like he could go on? His mother sat at the kitchen table looking out the same window and wondered what spring would be like this year without him.

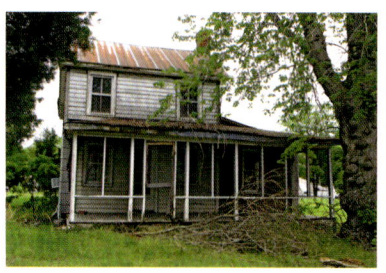

Did I ever tell you about my cousin, Maudie,
and the seven possums in the hen house?

GRANDPOP USED TO SIT THERE in that old porch chair and tell the kids one story after another about the "good ol' days." They knew he probably made half the stuff up, but they loved to listen. Funny thing about his stories—the endings kept changing. And seemed like he was always the hero. Like he was the star of his life. In his stories, Grandpop was always getting somebody out of a scrape. And he never failed to point out that it was foolishness, stupidity, or pig-headed obstinacy that got the person into the scrape. That was no doubt supposed to be a lesson to the kids, but they saw it as pure entertainment. He'd do the different voices and add sound effects and create suspense 'til all of them were just sitting there with their jaws hanging open, big eyes glued on him. Grandpop wasn't always as upbeat as his stories though. They never knew when the dark moods would take him. As a young man, he and his best friend, Sam, had gone off to war together to fight the Germans. Grandpop came back full of stories but left Sam lying in a field in France. Maybe all those stories about the folks he rescued had something to do with the one he couldn't save.

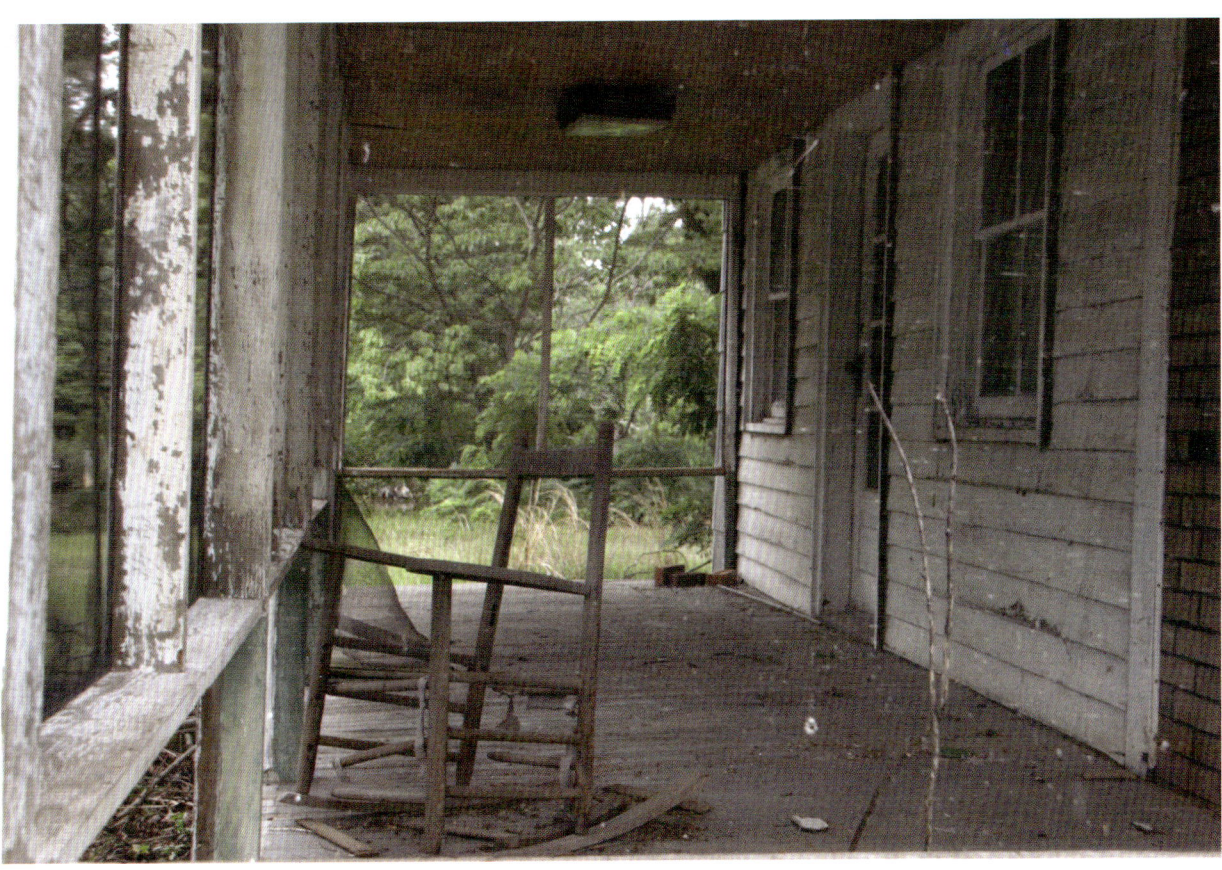

On Hungerford Creek.

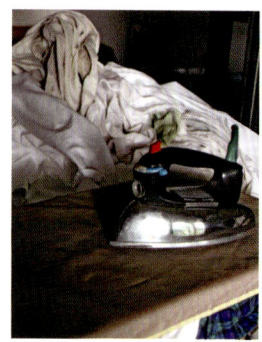

Pearl, leave those dishes and come to bed!
I got something for you . . .

"SHUSH," SHE SAID, mortified that the children might have heard. They always had a good time in bed when they got down to it, but she was tired after working all day in other folks' houses, then coming home to her own kids and the supper to cook. There was a pile of laundry so big it was starting to haunt her dreams. He worked hard, too, Lord knows, always out on the water or in the fields early and late. Most times, he was asleep by the time she got to bed. But tonight he stayed awake waiting for her, and he managed to make her forget her weariness long enough. Then, they both fell back in the bed and slept deep.

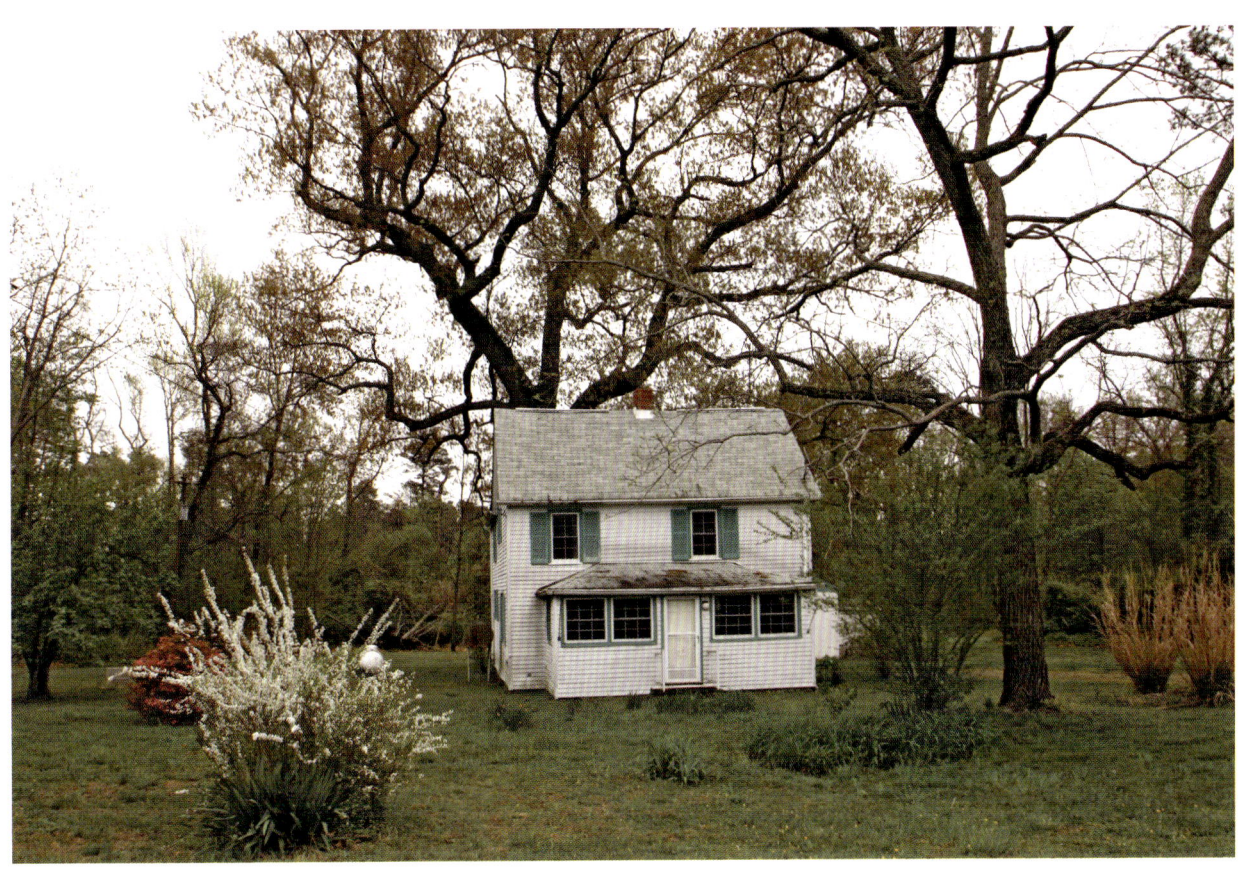

Ridge area.

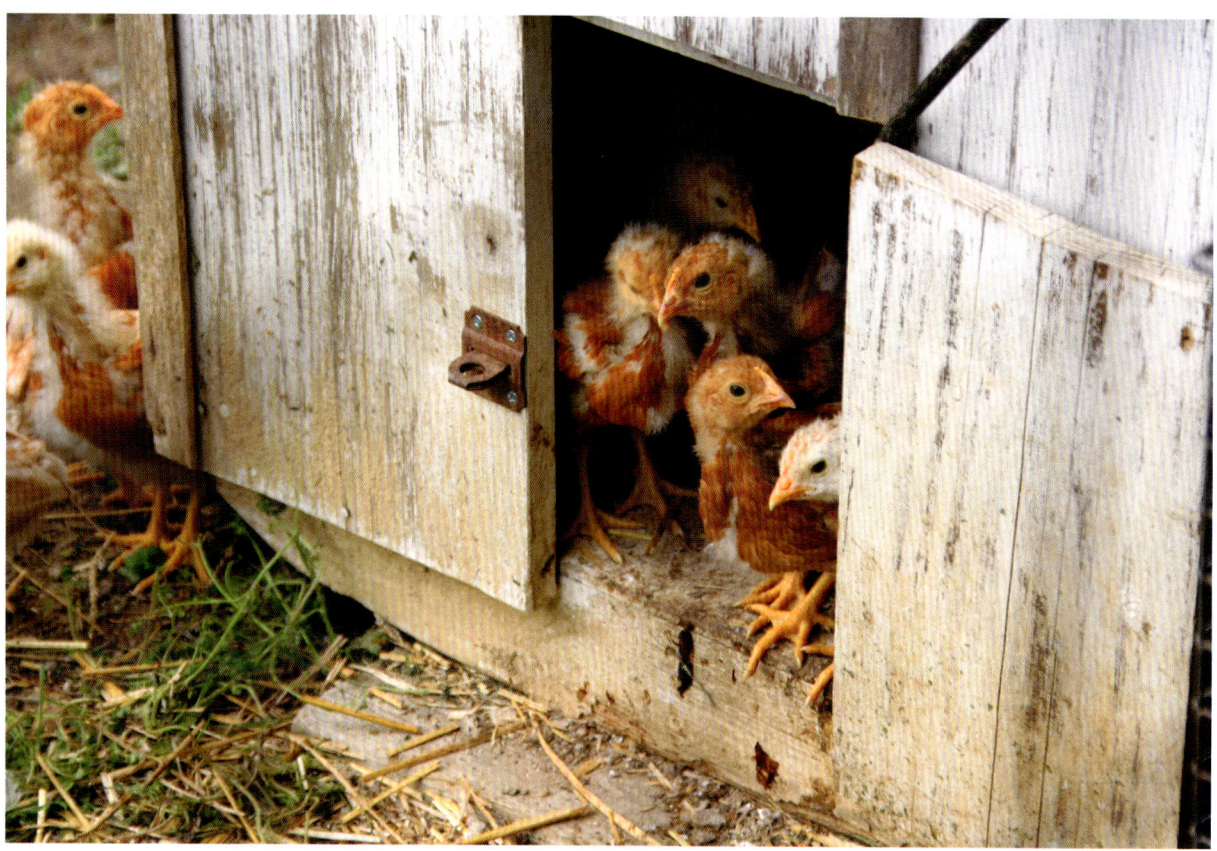

Brooder house.

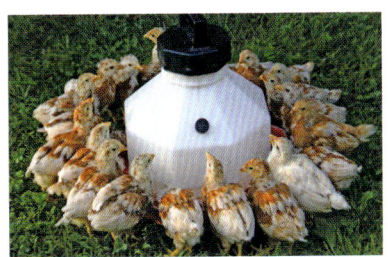

Here chick, chick, chick . . .

MACY TOSSED A LITTLE FOOD TOWARD THE CHICKS and laughed when they crowded around the feeder. She got a kick out of their enthusiasm and squabbling, heads bobbing up and down as they ate and drank. The sounds the hens made when they spotted a juicy-looking bug or announced their daily accomplishment of laying an egg amused her, and she could always get a laugh from her younger brothers and sisters by imitating the various clucks and squawks. She stood a moment admiring the new brooder house her Uncle Rob had built for the chicks. It was well worth having chickens, she thought, as she entered the henhouse to collect the beautiful light-brown eggs. They asked little and gave a lot.

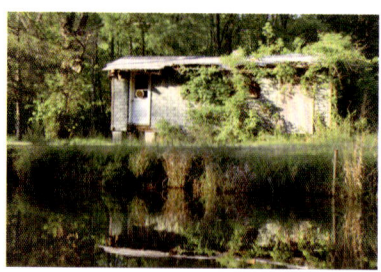

John Henry, hush up, boy. Give it a rest.
Them foxes don't need you barkin' along with 'em.

THE DOG GAVE A COUPLE MORE WOOFS as he circled and settled down again. The man was tired from his dawn-to-dusk work in the tobacco fields and needed rest. He had heated up some squirrel stew on the gas burner, given the dog a portion, and finished the rest. He sat at the small table for a little while studying a scrap of newspaper in the light of his lantern. His eyes roamed the page. A news brief suggested: "Tired of wisteria? Try the kudzu vine." He moved on to a story about a shooting and an account of a bus boycott going on down in Alabama. He shook his head over an ad telling him he could rent a new Pontiac for $300 down and $18 a week. Wouldn't he just like to have that kind of money?! He turned down the lantern wick, blew it out, patted the dog on the head, and rolled on to his cot.

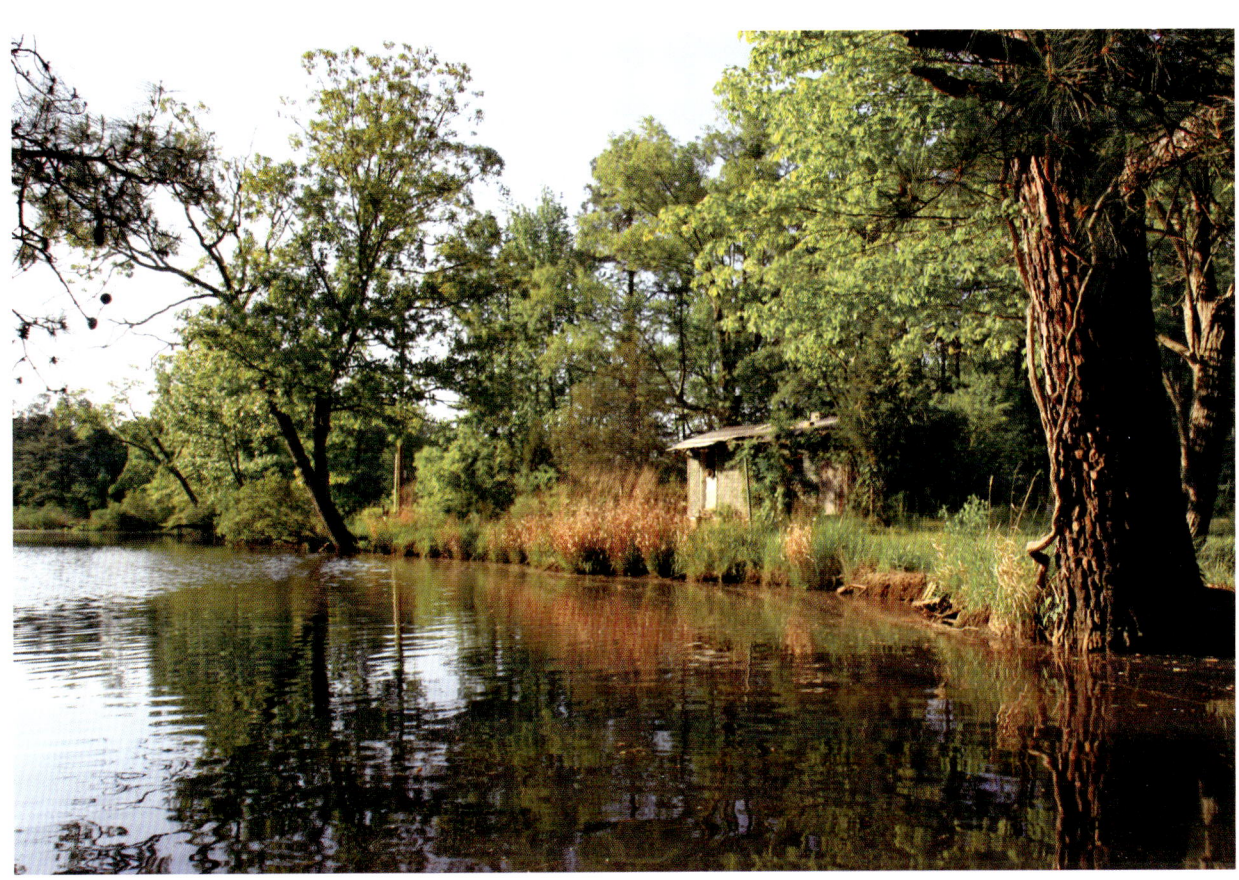

Along the St. Mary's River.

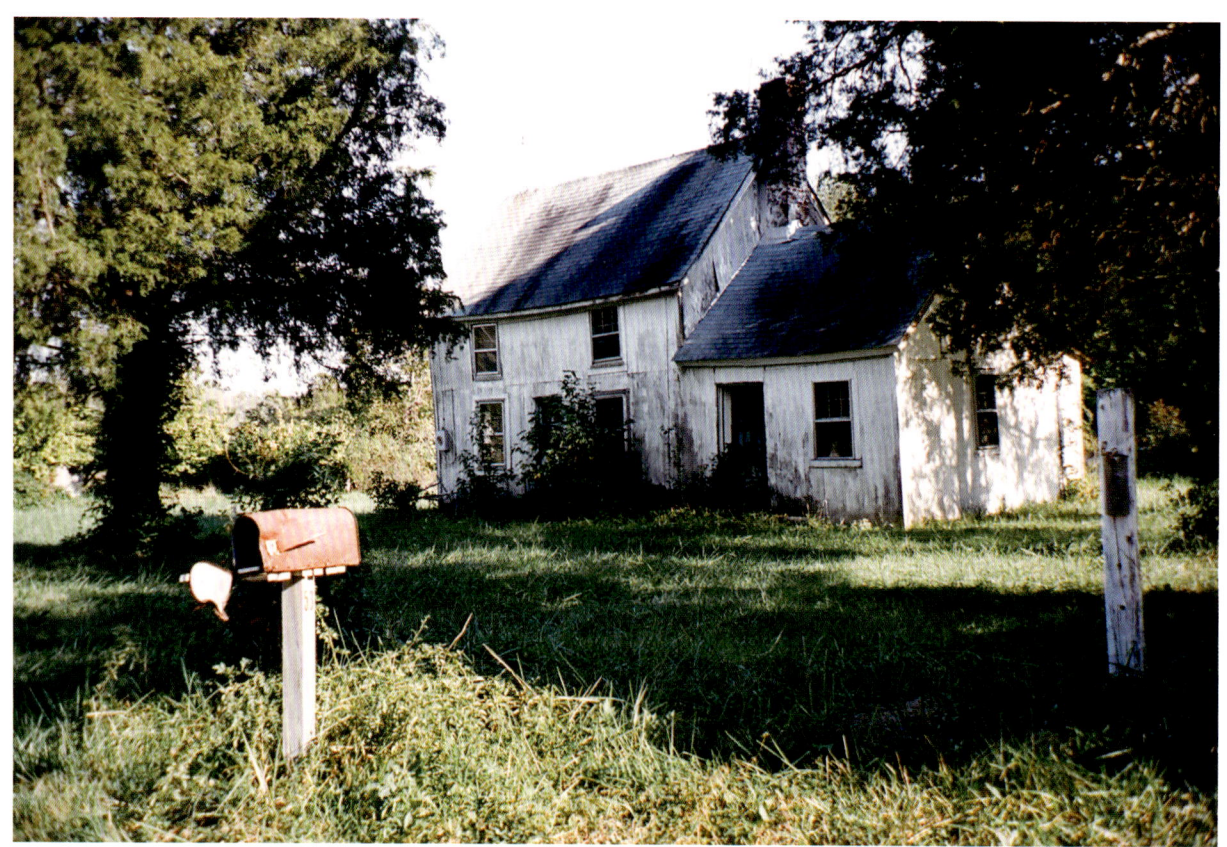

Beachville.

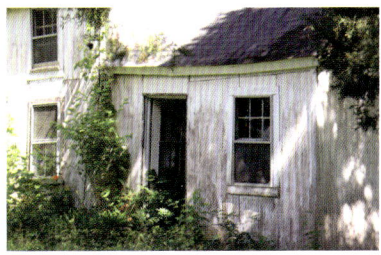

Jack Sprat could eat no fat. His wife could eat no lean . . .

THE FIRST TIME HE REMEMBERED HER chanting the rhyme was when he had insisted on trying to carry her across the threshold the day they came home from their honeymoon. She outweighed him by almost sixty pounds, and the attempt was doomed to failure. They stumbled through the door and fell to the floor laughing almost hysterically as she gasped out the nursery rhyme. She stayed heavy and robust over the years. He stayed slim in spite of eating her delicious pies and cakes and stuffed ham, though he did develop a bit of a paunch as his hair began to gray. "More to love," she'd say, and, of course, he had to agree with her. When the cancer struck, the weight seemed to fall away from her by the day, until her body barely seemed to make an impression in the bed. When at last they carried her out the door, she was light as a feather, and Jack couldn't help but feel the bitter irony of it.

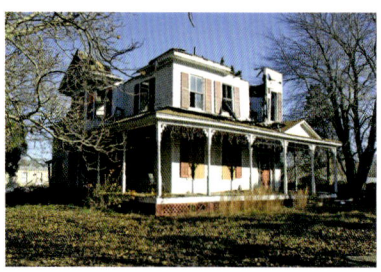

*Come on and sit down everybody, before the biscuits get cold and
your dad blows a gasket. Now, whose turn is it to say grace?*

THE RESPONSIBILITY OF SAYING GRACE was closely regulated in the family,
and even the littlest one was expected to contribute as soon as words
could be formed and reasonably understood. Eating time was family time,
and attendance was not optional. Father sat at the head of the long, polished
oak table and Mother at the foot. Three children sat on one side and two
children and a spinster aunt on the other. Only after everyone was seated,
hands in laps and eyes cast down, was grace offered. Following a heartfelt
"Amen," the meat platter was handed to Father for his perusal and selection.
That he should be served first was without question. Father considered himself a beneficent master of all he surveyed, whether at the dinner table or the
bank in town where he served as manager. All he asked of both his business
and household was that they be run in an orderly and respectable fashion.
This did not seem to him to be an unreasonable request.

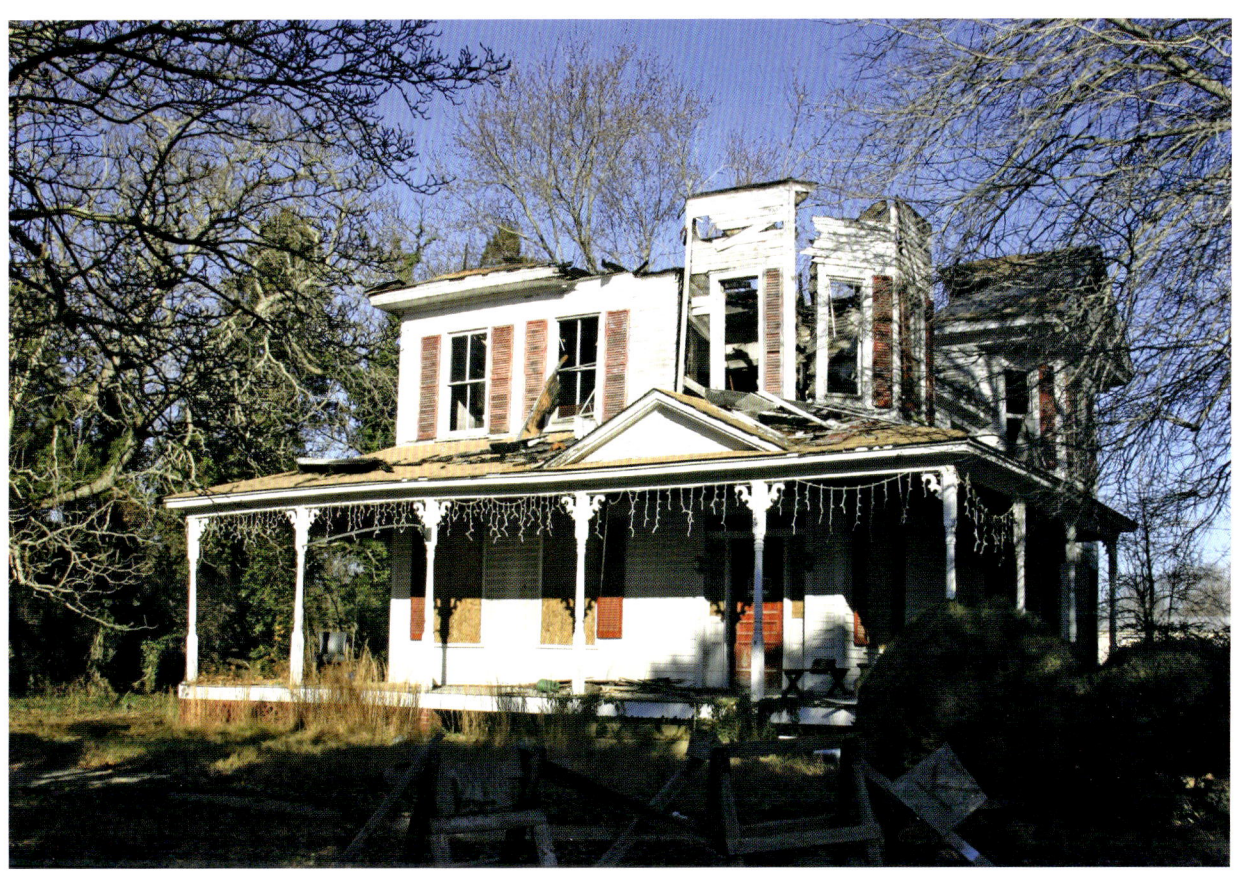

Point Lookout Road.

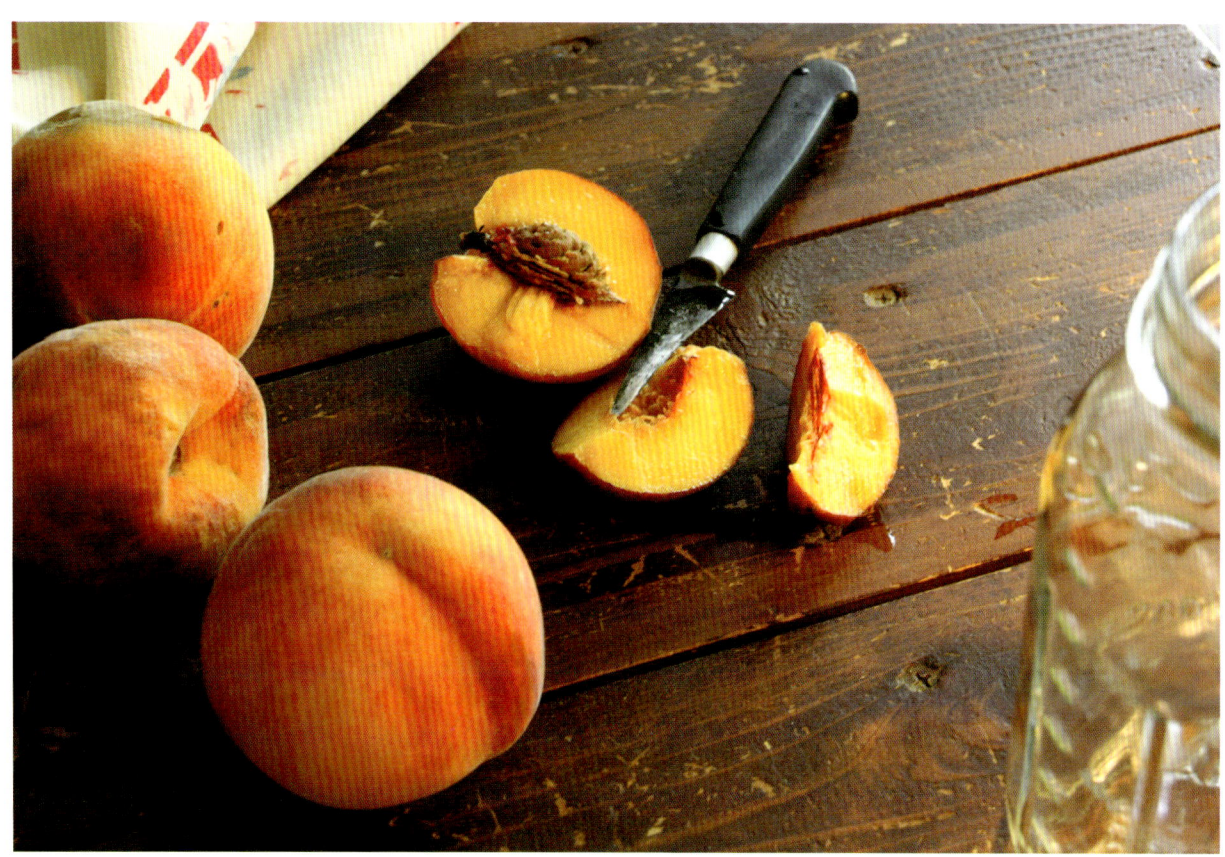

Canning local peaches.

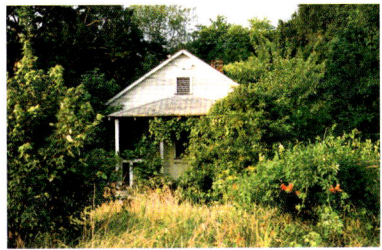

Baby girl, you best stop putting every other one in your mouth or you be getting a bellyache and wearing out the path to the outhouse.

S HE WAS SPEAKING TO THE LITTLEST ONE of the five kids sitting around the table, peeling the peaches. They had gotten two big boxes of bruised fruit that the farmer down in Ridge was getting rid of cheap, and a mound of peels and pits was growing in the center of the table. The big black-enameled canner was rumbling, and the steam fogged up her glasses as she lifted off the lid and raised the rack. She was glad to have the older girls home from school to help. Dot was too young to be much use yet. They had a mess of beans to do today, too. She was hard on the kids, but that was the way it was when she was coming up. She'd sat right there in that same kitchen doing up tomatoes for days with her mother chiding her to pick up the pace. But just wait 'til the kids taste those peaches with thick cream she'd spoon off the milk come January, she thought, smiling to herself.

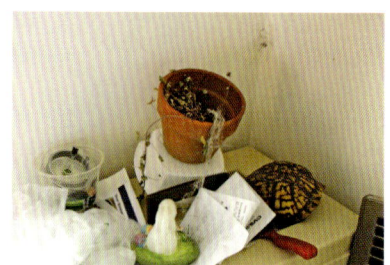

Shoot. This place looks like a pig sty. Why don't you get off
your butt and do some work around here instead of watching
your soaps all day and drinking my beer?

I T WAS TRUE, when you looked around the house, things were a mess.
Stacks of magazines and old newspapers, discarded mail, and even a long-
dead potted plant were piled in the corners. The faded carpet was filthy with
ground-in crumbs in front of the sofa where she sat. The dingy porcelain
sink was piled high with dirty dishes. Last night's plates still sat on the table,
where one of the cats was, at that moment, busy licking off the remains of
sausage grease. The woman seemed stuck in a holding pattern, powerless to
move forward or back. Both of them, caught in this moment that would not
turn into something different.

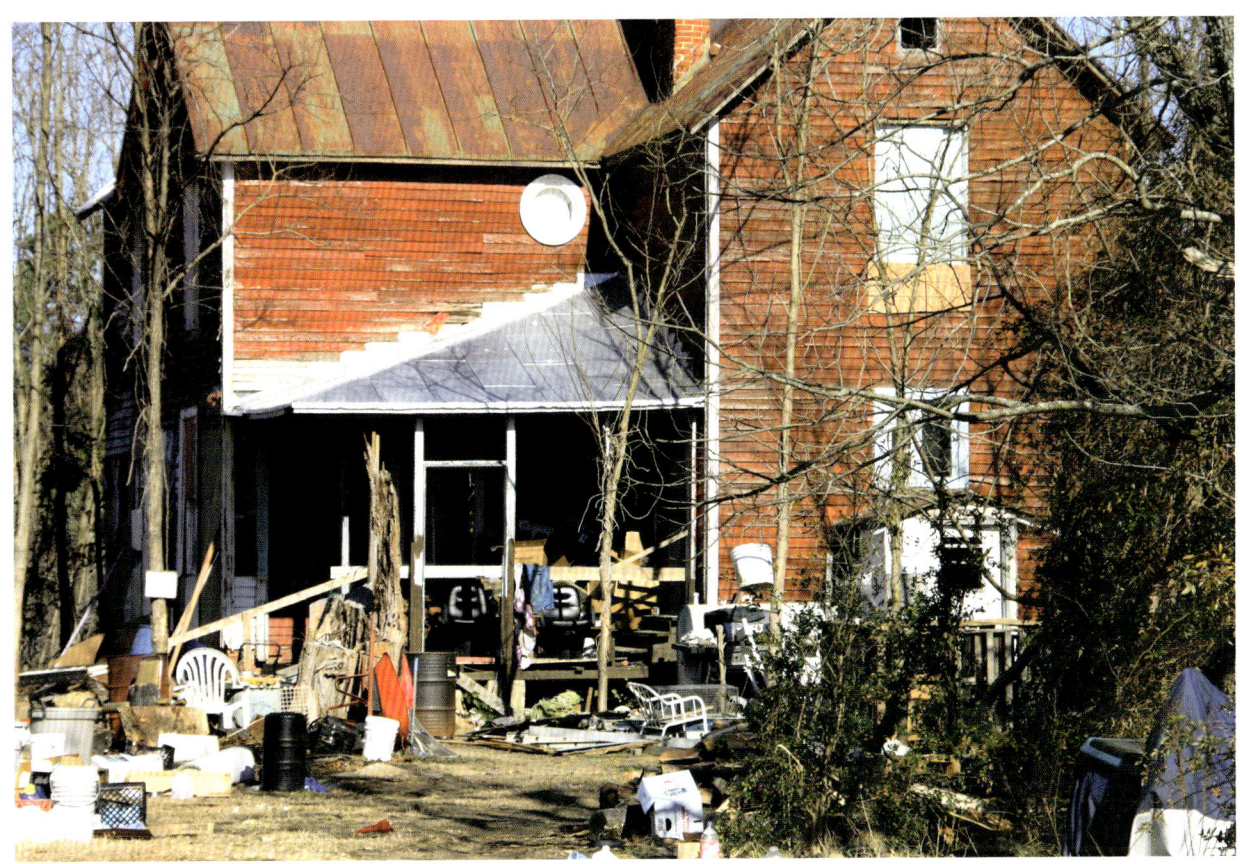

Great Mills area.

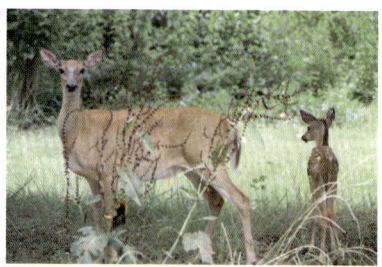

Jacob, come look! Look at that fawn!

ROSE STOOD LOOKING OUT THE WINDOW, her hand suspended above the dishwater, and marveled at the tiny spotted creature. It couldn't be more than a few days old, she thought, the youngest she'd seen this spring. She placed her hand on the roundness of her belly and wondered if the new life growing within her was the reason she felt moved almost to tears as she watched the incredibly fragile-looking fawn standing there in the patch of sun by the garden fence. The fawn moved off slowly, following its mother, then suddenly sprang out of sight. Rose smiled at herself and bent her head back to the breakfast dishes.

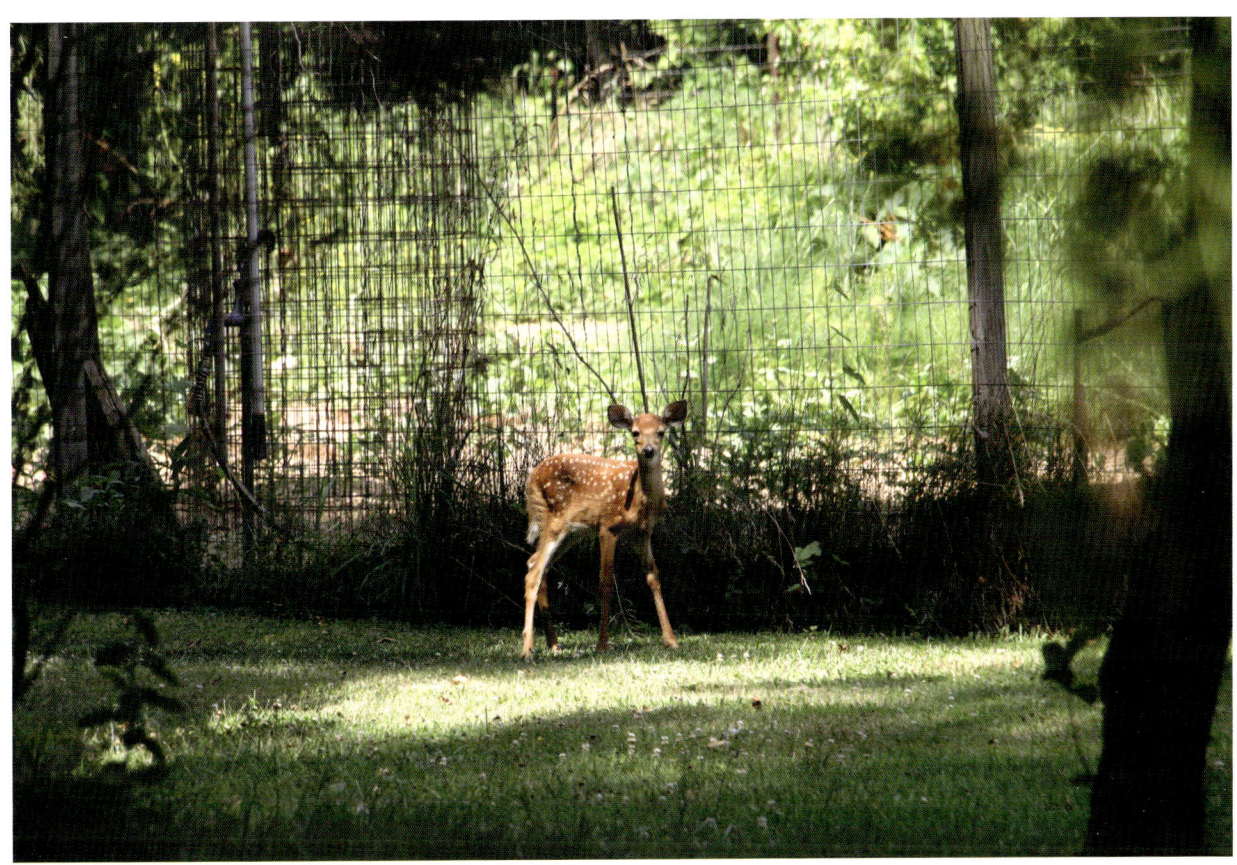

Fawn at the garden fence.

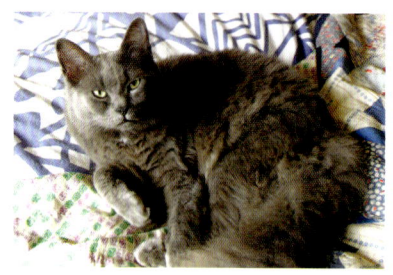

Now, where did I put my glasses? Lordy,
I'll be losing the nose off my face next.

Her bones were fragile now, and her joints were achy with arthritis, but she clung to all her daily routines with the tenacity of the stubborn old women she was. And when the day was especially fine, she'd still get in her little skiff and poke around the creek, do some crabbing. Living alone suited her just fine. She had her TV programs and her daily crossword, and she'd listen to the talk shows on the radio and shake her head at the foolishness of some people. There was Gerald, her cat, and the only male she'd ever really taken a liking to. But if she really got to feeling lonely, she'd call up Ethel, her neighbor one block over, and the two of them would walk over to Mattingly's and get some coffee or walk along the little boardwalk in town, feed the ducks, and maybe get an ice cream. She didn't have extra, but her money stretched just far enough. She really should find a man to do a little fixing on the house, though, she thought. Get it nice and tight for winter.

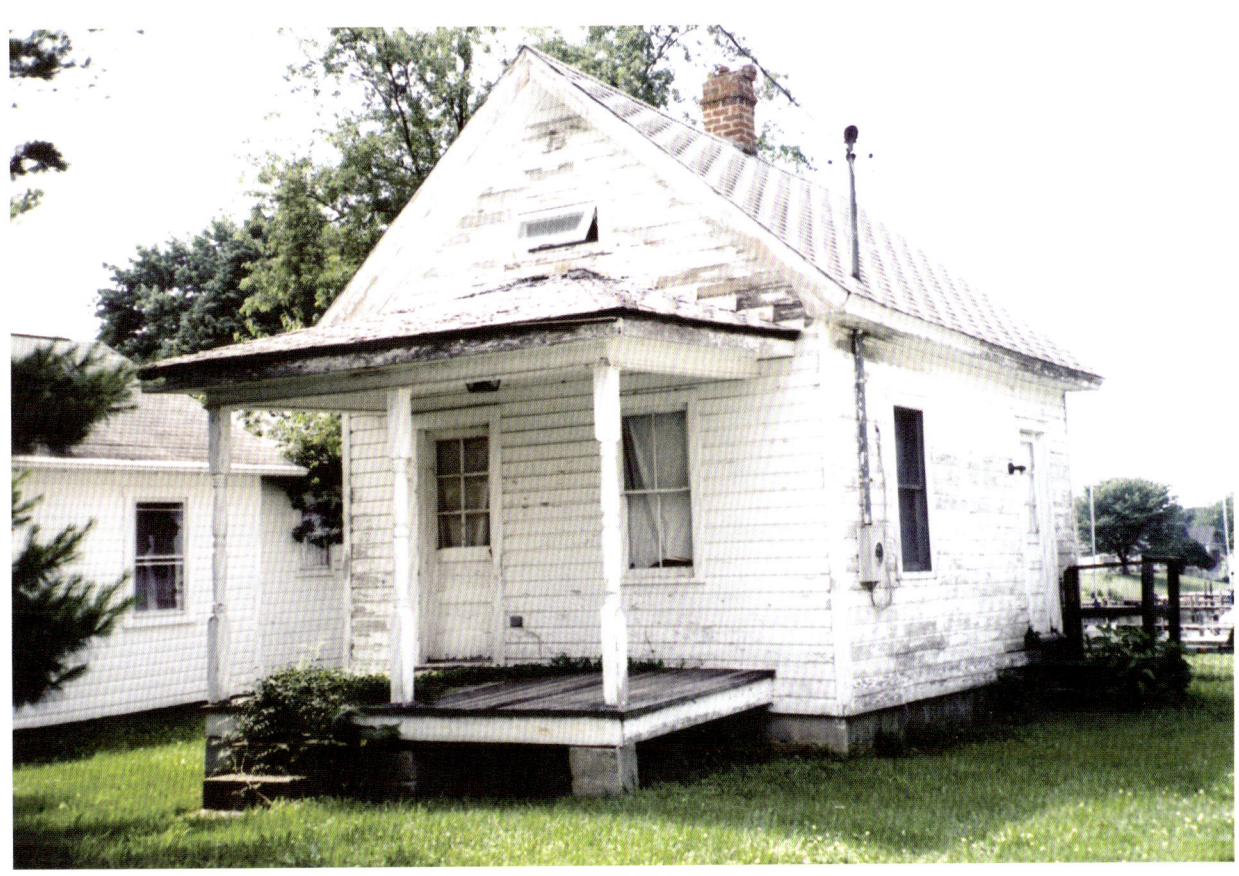

Solomon's Island.

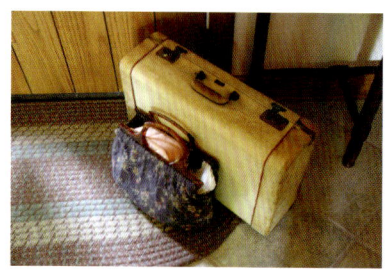

Oh, my Lord. Benny! Run down to the barn
and tell your dad to come NOW. It's time.

IT WAS THREE WEEKS EARLY, but her hospital bags were packed, and her mom was more or less on call, ready to come help out, she said, at least for a few weeks. With all these kids and one still in diapers, she really needed all the help she could get. Not that her husband didn't try. But there was the farm to run, and he needed the boys to help him. That was the way it was supposed to work, wasn't it? Have all these kids so you had many hands to lighten the load? Nanny Gough had been there to birth the first three at home. She wished the quiet, stern old woman hadn't given it up. The contractions were getting stronger. Make this one come quick and easy, she prayed to whoever might be listening. She turned off the fire under the soup pot, picked up her bags, and headed out to the truck. Where *was* that man?

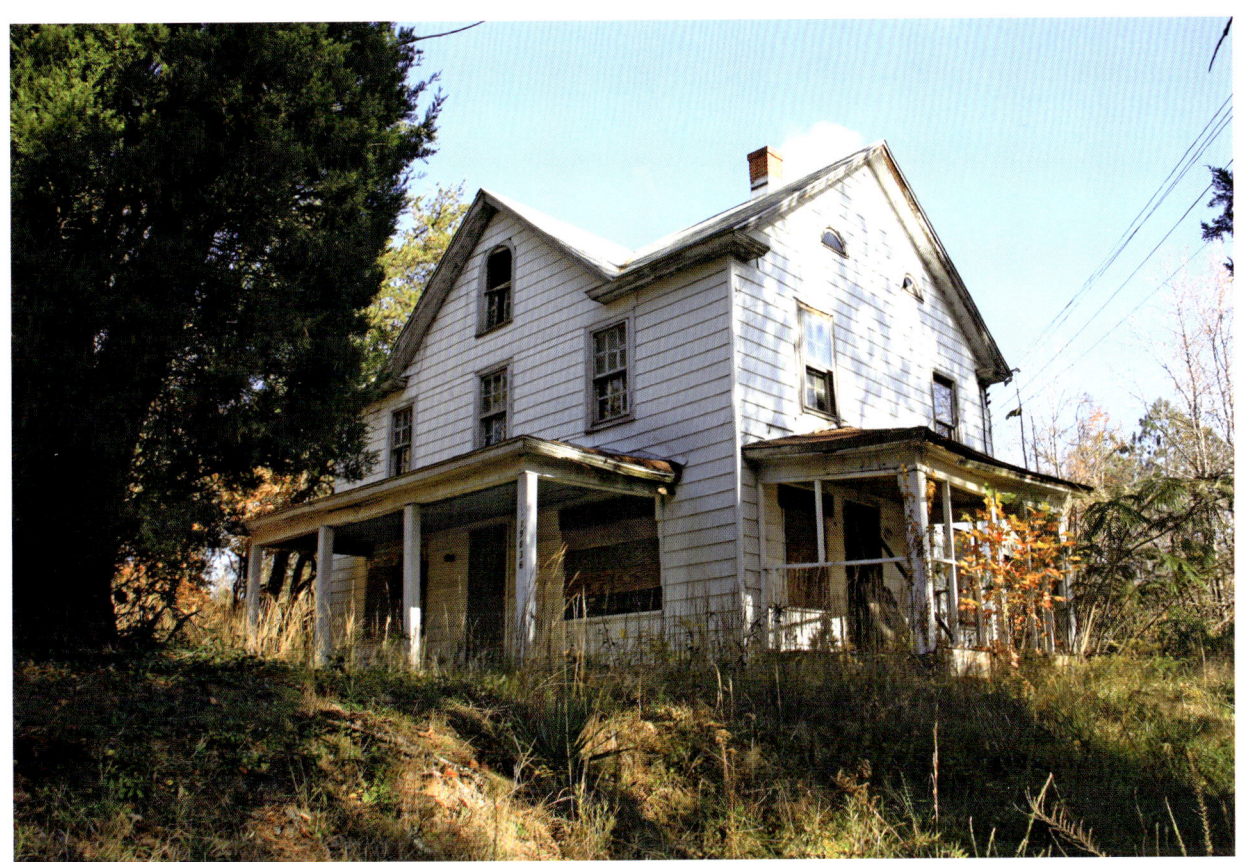

Callaway.

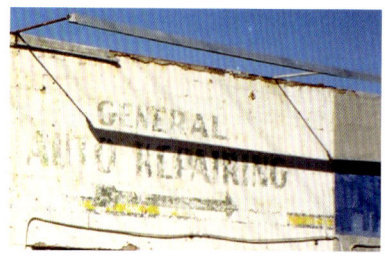

Your truck's ready, Tim, but what we got here is a good-news,
bad-news situation. Which you want first?

Buddy didn't really have any good news, at least not anything that was going to soften the blow much. He'd been working on that old truck, trying to keep it on the road for Tim for so many years he felt like it was an old friend. And he was about to pronounce a death sentence. It just wasn't worth putting the money into it, even if Tim had it, which he knew he didn't. All he could do to try and help him look on the bright side was tell him about the sale going on at Bell Motors and the good terms he heard they were offering on new pickups.

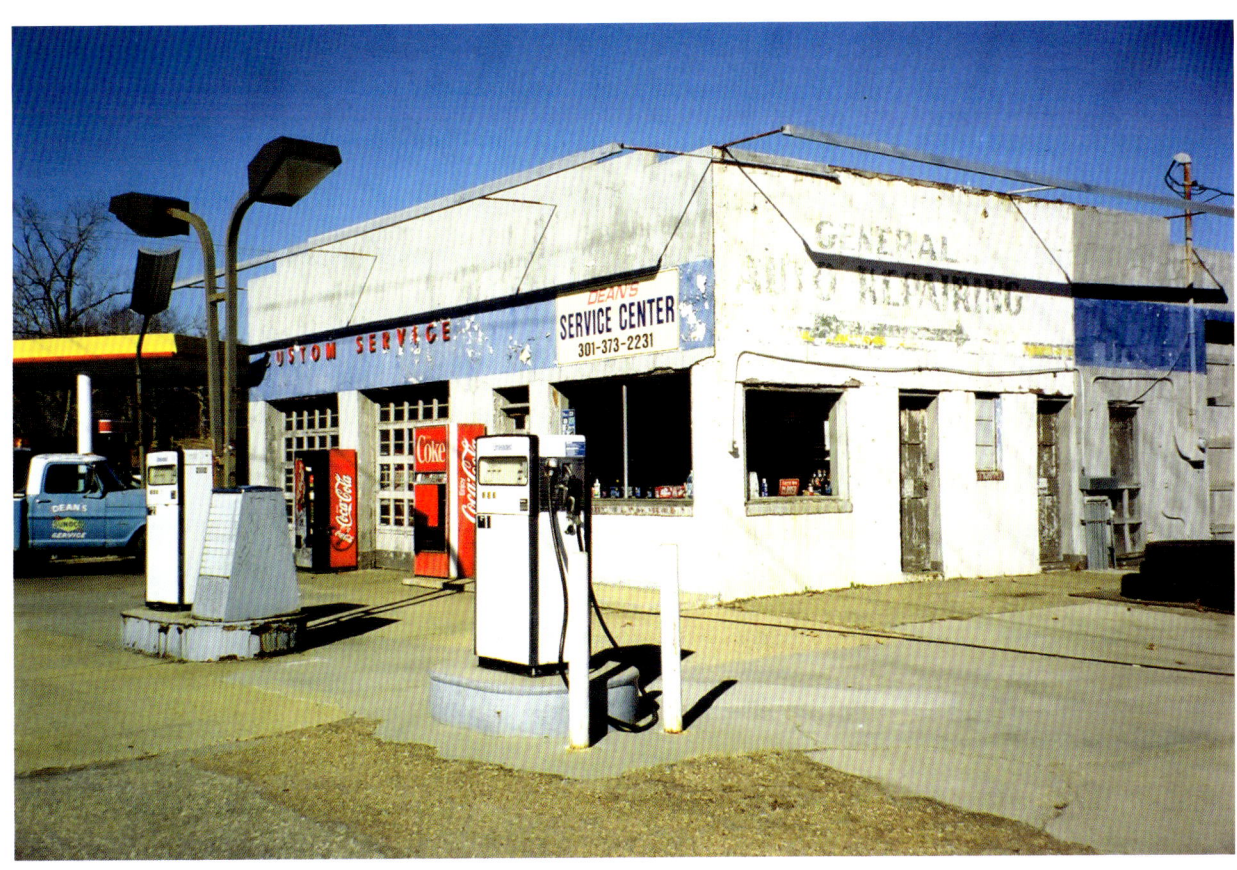

Along Maryland Route 235 (Three Notch Road) in Hollywood.

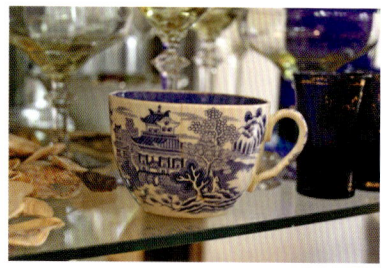

There!

THE DAY AFTER HIS EIGHTY-SEVENTH BIRTHDAY, Eldon gazed with satisfaction at the mended cup he had gently placed in the china cabinet.
His heart had almost stopped when he felt it slip from his soapy hand and
crack as it hit the edge of the sink. *Eldon!* He heard his long-dead mother's
voice as clear as if she was standing beside him. The blue-and-white bone
china had been a wedding gift to her mother and father and was precious to
her. More precious, he often thought, than the feelings of the over-sensitive,
awkward boy child he felt himself still to be.

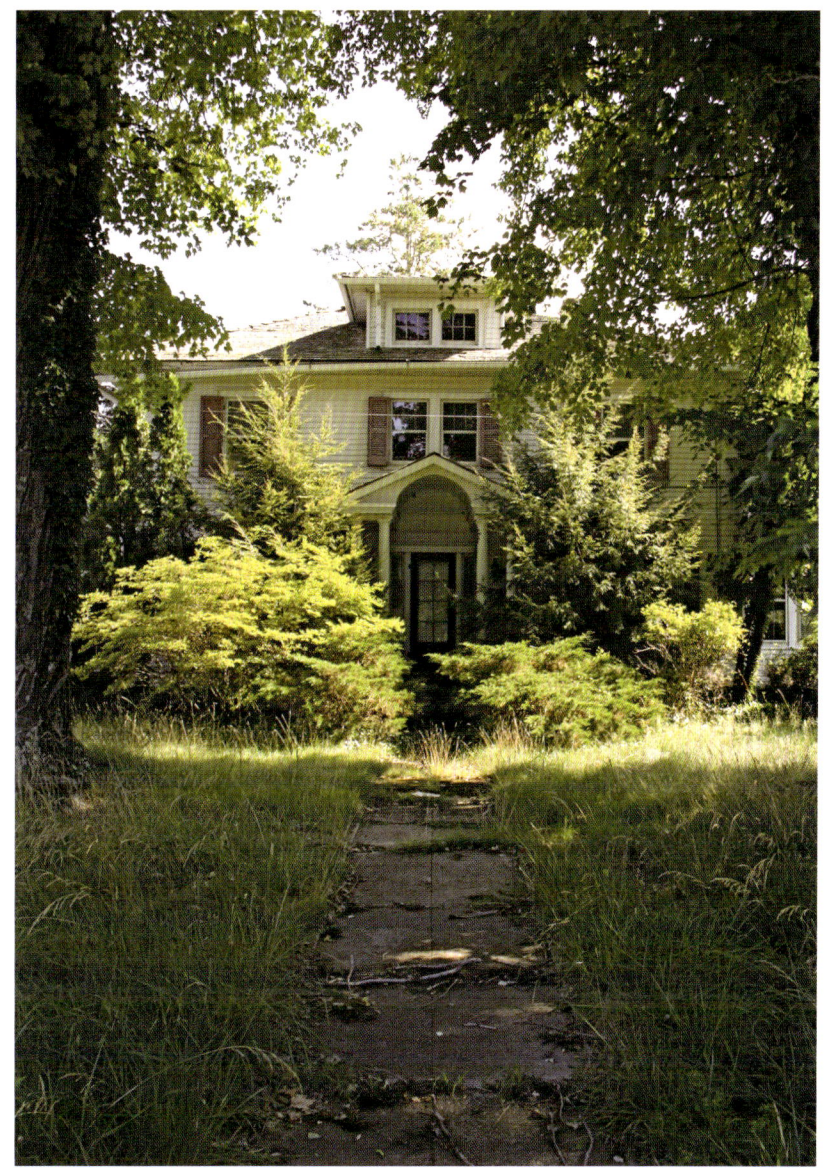

Great Mills area.

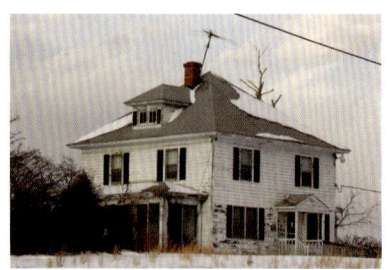

Knit one, purl one, knit two together . . .

MARION AND HER HUSBAND sat at opposite ends of the living room, she with knitting needles flying, he with the newspaper on his lap, head dropped back and mouth open. A light snore and the click of the needles were the only sounds in the room. Marion closed her eyes, letting her hands drop with a sigh. If only, she thought for the thousandth time, his love for her had been large enough to fit in a child. The hurt was old and familiar but a hurt nonetheless. She sighed, gave her head a little shake, and carried on with her knitting.

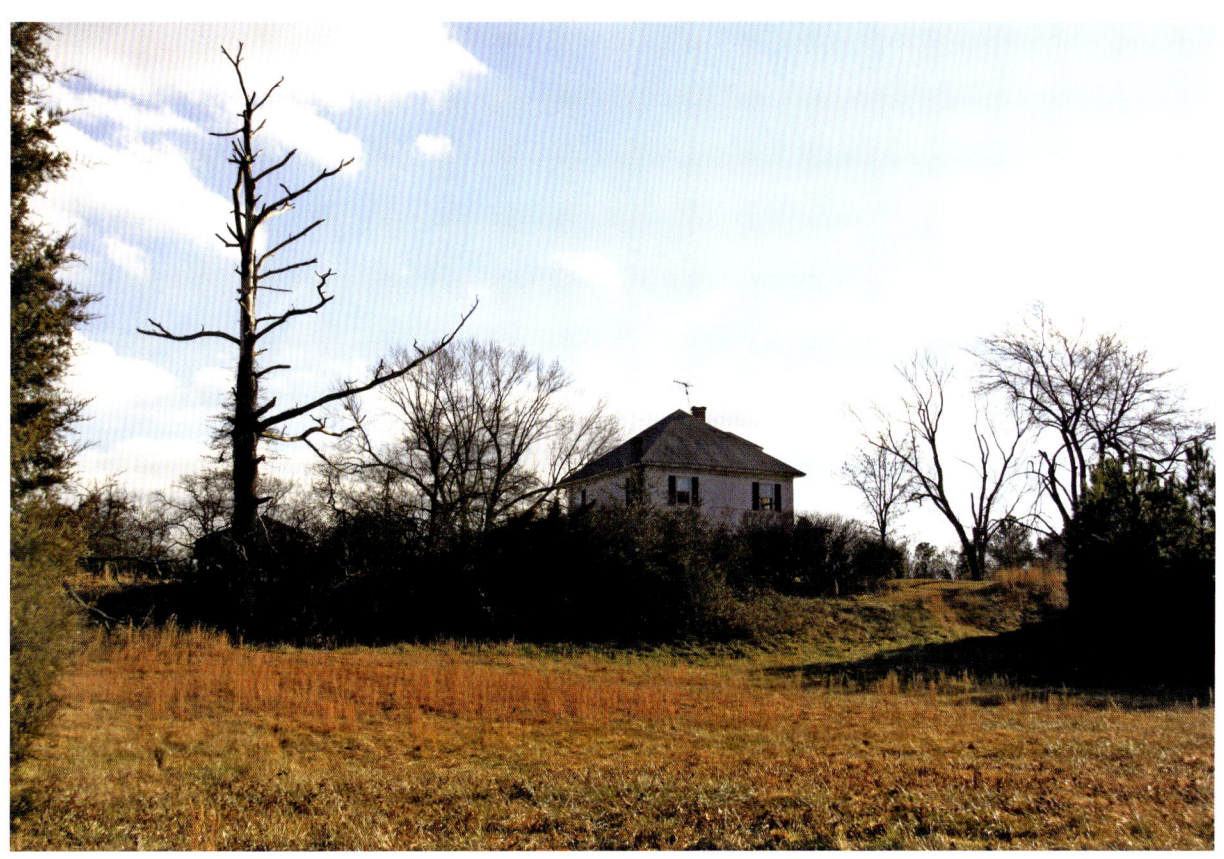

Old Three Notch Road.

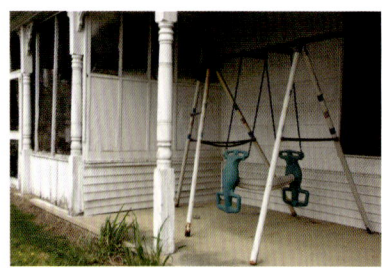

Well, Mae, looks like you and Joe are going to be
welcoming another little one come April.

As Doc Green packed up his bag, Mae hung her head and shivered, feeling chilled to the bone even in the late summer heat. "Come on now, give us a smile, dear." He knew Mae felt no joy at the prospect of another mouth to feed but didn't want to encourage her blues. The best he could do for her was to help usher in a healthy child. The rest was in God's hands. She'd just have to bear up and accept it with what grace she could muster.

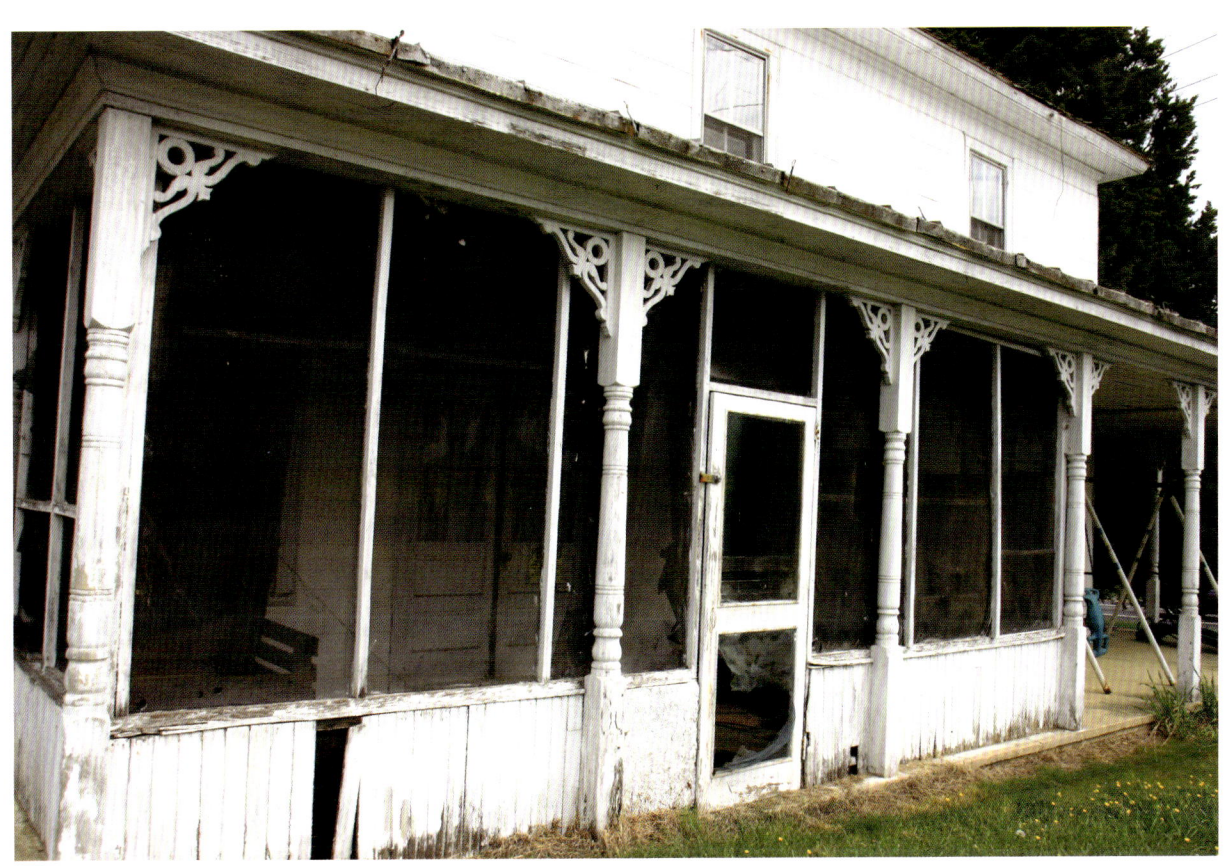

Medley's Neck Road.

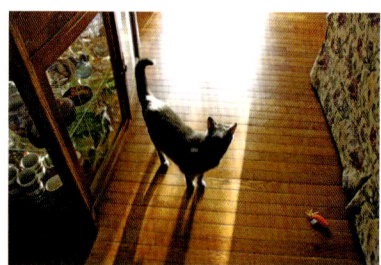

Aunt Margie, why do you have all these weird things in with the pretty things?

MARGIE HAD ALWAYS LOVED ROCKS AND SHELLS and interesting drift-wood. Even as a child she had always come home from a visit to the beach with pockets full of treasures. She didn't see these things as any less beautiful or deserving of a place of honor than her family heirlooms. Now that she had only herself to please, her "finds" were starting to crowd out the cups and saucers. She left the colored glass in place, though, because she loved how it caught the morning sun. That was one thing that wasn't so bad about being on her own. Her nieces and nephews might think she was a little peculiar, but that didn't bother her a bit.

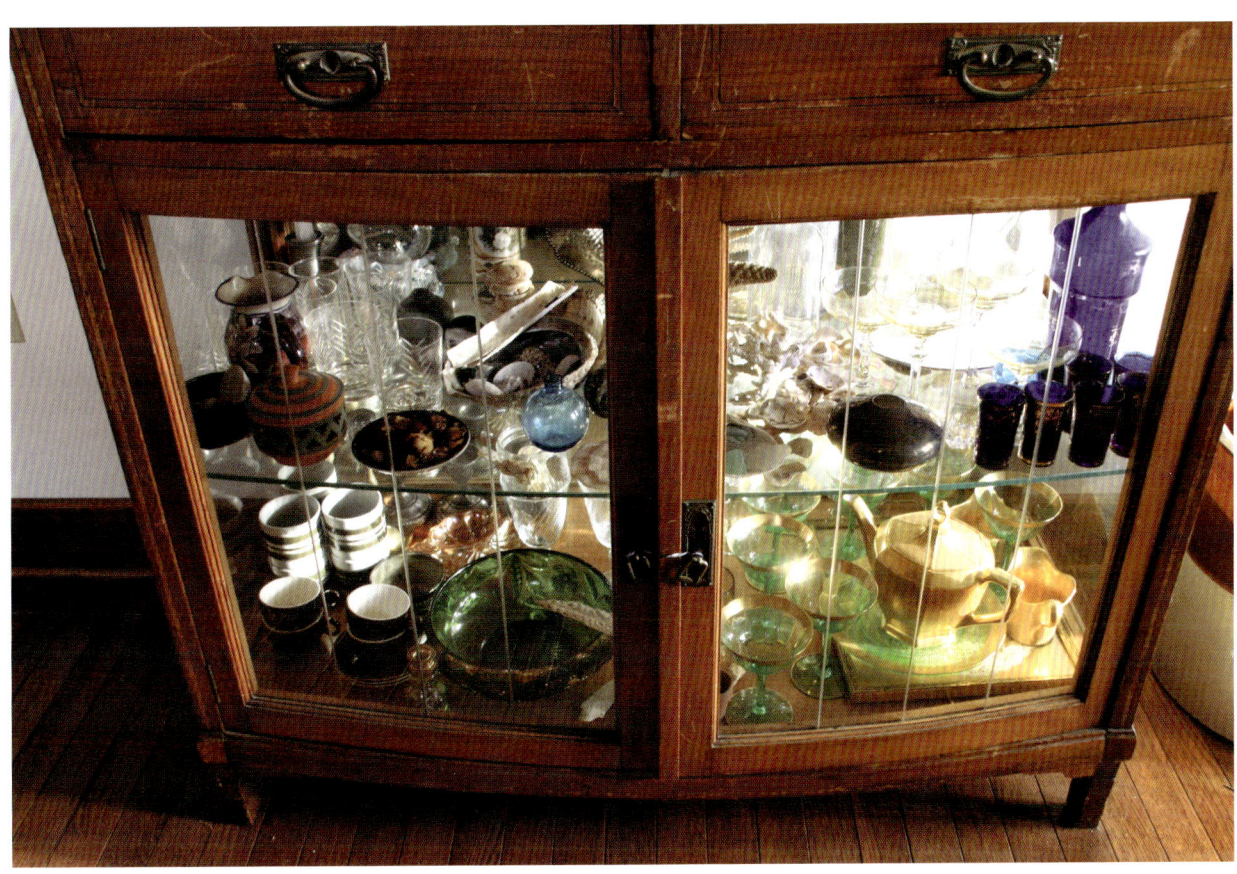

Vintage oak china cabinet.

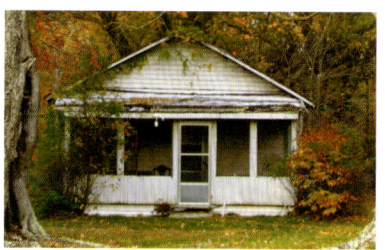

Jamie, turn that TV off now! Your dad's gonna be shaking
you out the bed before daylight, and you need your rest.

THE BOY GOT UP SLOWLY, dragging his feet toward the bedroom. As he lay down, thinking about what the morning would bring, he felt excited but worried, too. He'd been practicing with the shotgun plenty and figured he'd be a good enough shot when the chance came. He looked forward to being out there in the early-morning woods with his dad. But when he pictured that deer right there in his sites and imagined squeezing the trigger . . . well, he just wasn't so sure.

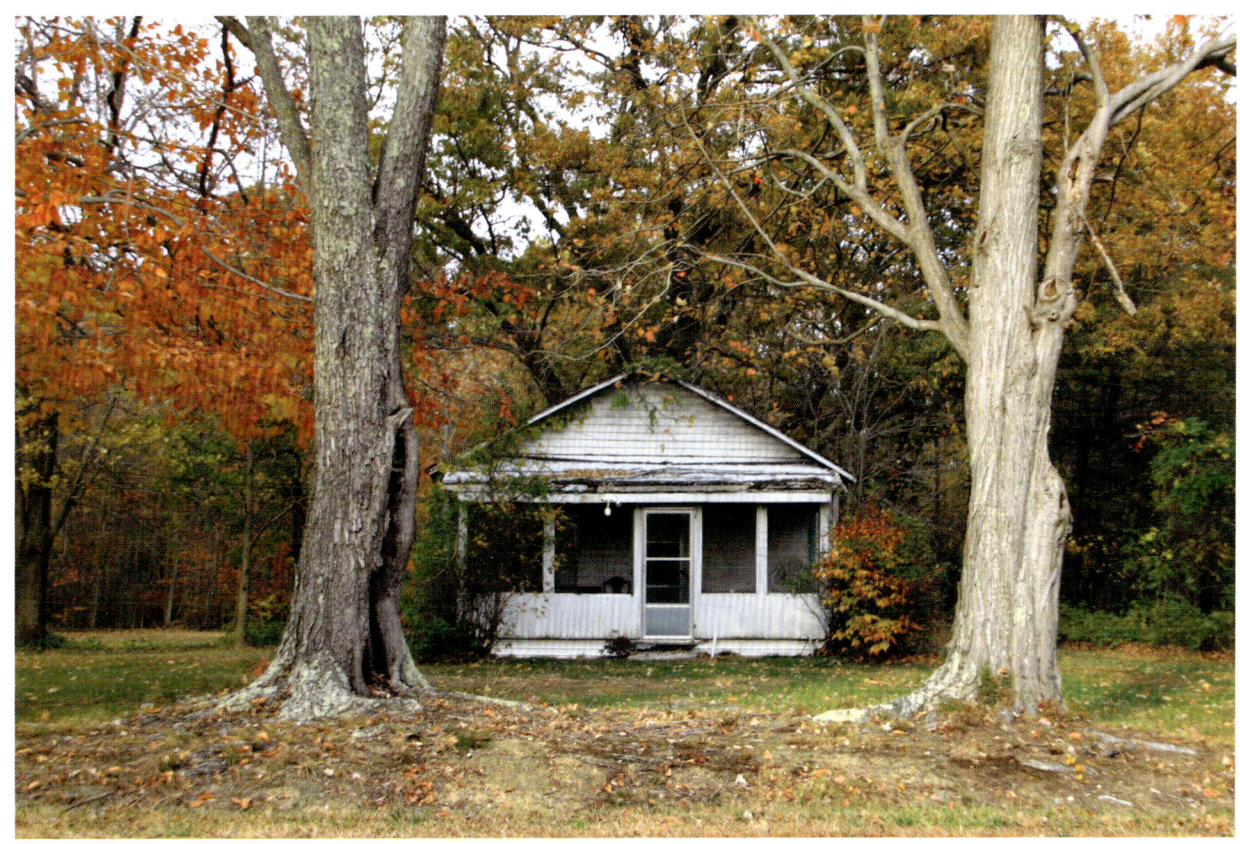

Budds Creek area.

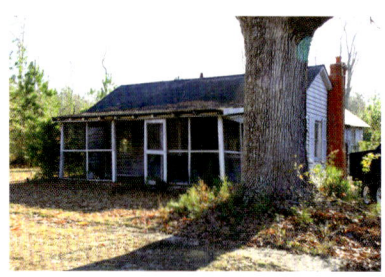

I'm cold.

THE LITTLE BOY PULLED THE THIN, scratchy blanket up to his chin, wishing it was his turn to sleep in the warm middle spot where his sister was. His brother, sleeping on the other side of the skinny bed, hissed, "Shut up, would ya?" All three kids longed for spring so they could sleep outdoors some. They had an old tent that would keep out most of the skeeters. But warm weather was months away still. On bitter cold nights like these, they'd get ready for bed by backing up close as they could to the woodstove, and then, when their clothes were just about scorched, they'd all run and hop into bed. But that stove heat disappeared fast, and they were happy enough to have three bodies to warm the bed.

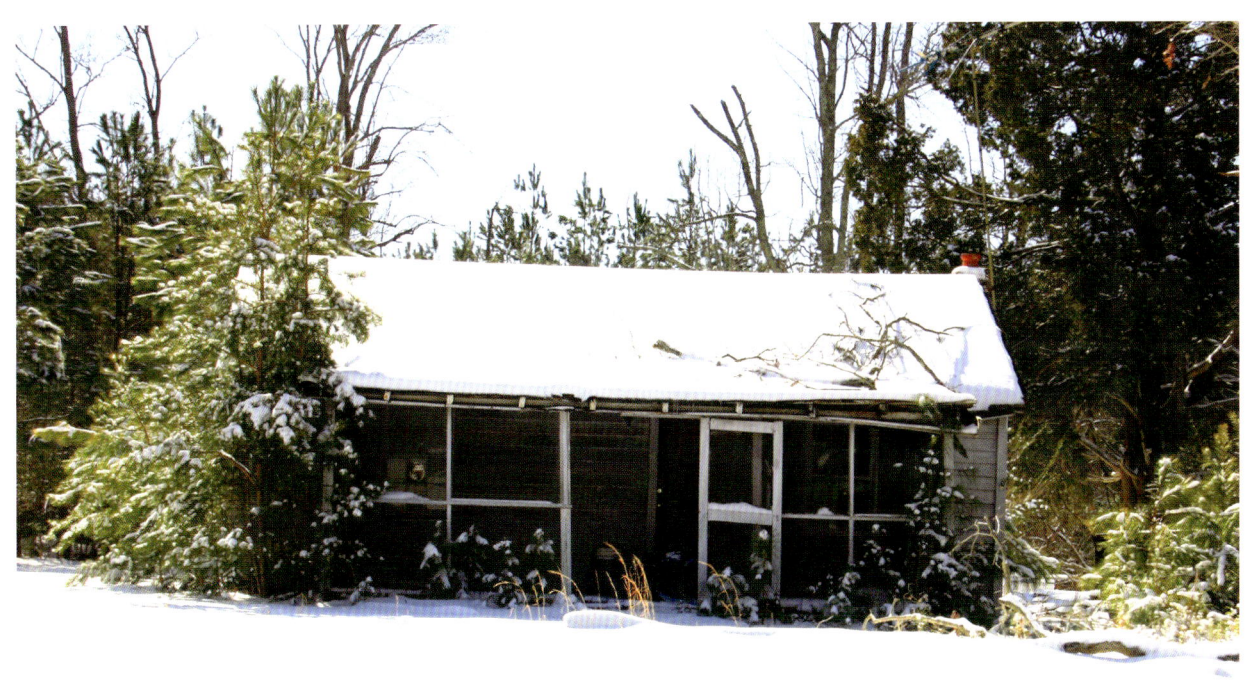

Park Hall Road.

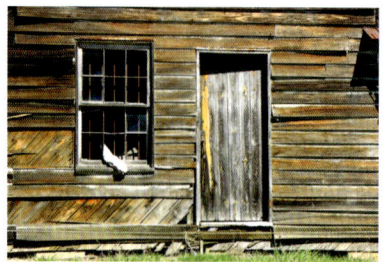

. . . And one more BB-Bat, a Bit-O-Honey, and a Kitts.

THEY HAD TAKEN A LONG TIME staring into the glass showcase before making up their minds and now watched with rapt attention as the old man filled the little brown penny-candy bag. The boy carefully laid his money on the counter and watched the old man snatch it up, put it in his cash drawer, and quickly toss the change back on the counter. No touching. He seemed to want them out the door and out of his hair as quick as could be. One time, when the man's daughter was minding the store, she had let them walk around and admire all the new garden and farm equipment and rows of seed packets, with their beautiful pictures of flowers and vegetables, before she'd said they'd better run on home.

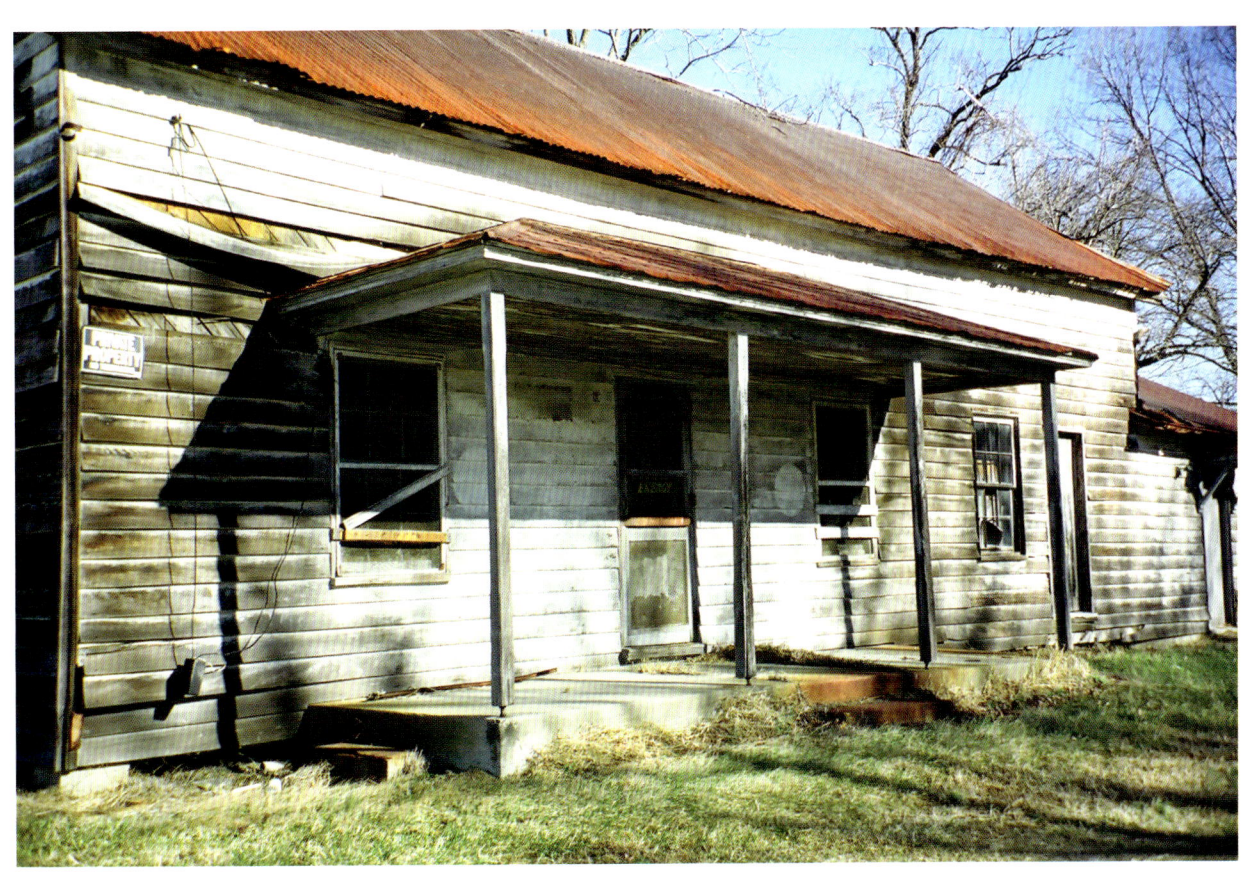

Old Bowles Store on Hollywood Road (no longer standing).

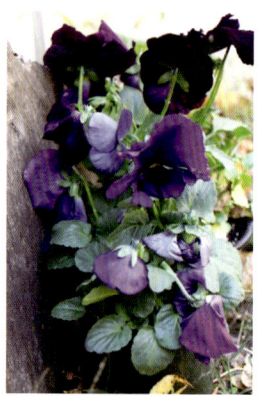

*Time to think about getting up to Hurry's store,
get us some seed potatoes, Lovey. Need to get
those in the ground next week.*

H<small>E LIKED TO GET HIS SEED POTATOES</small> in by St. Patty's Day. He bought them at the general store in Clements in the ten-pound brown sack. He'd pick up some onion sets and a few packets of seeds, too, depending on what was on sale. And he'd come back home, as he did every year, with some blue pansy plants for her to set out by the porch. He knew by now what she'd want, and he enjoyed seeing her smile as if surprised that he had thought to buy the pansies for her. She put the kettle on for tea every day at four o'clock, a habit she'd picked up from her English granny. When she'd set the plate of cookies on the table, he'd usually give her a peck on the cheek or sometimes give her hand a squeeze. That was their way, leaving a lot unsaid.

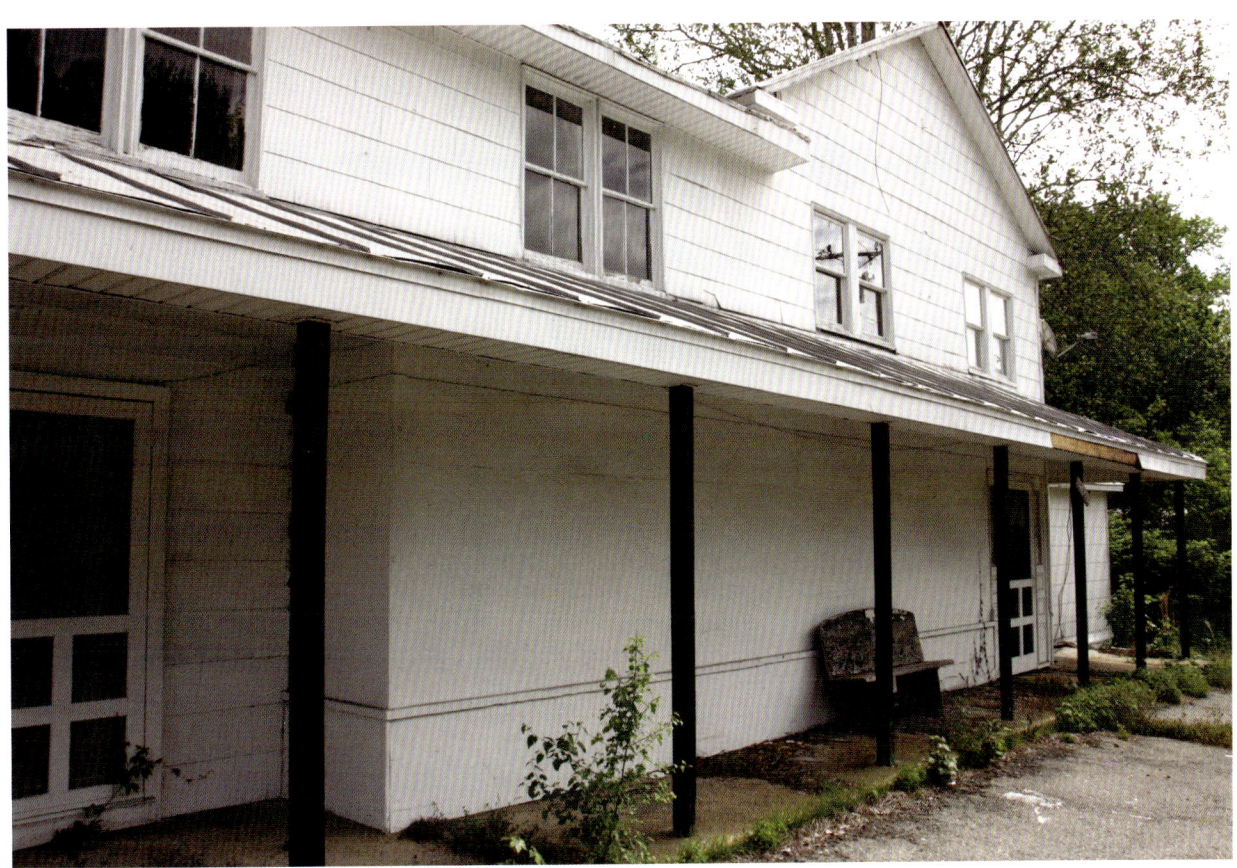

Hurry's Store in Clements.

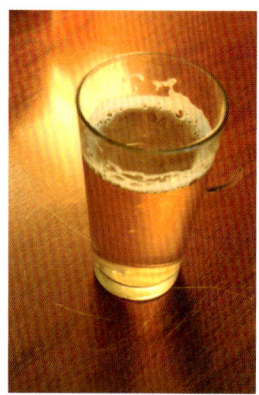

Turn that fan this way, Pete, and give me
whatever you got on tap, long as it's cold.

S ID SETTLED ON THE STOOL, propped his elbows on the bar, and soaked up
the relatively cool air and darkness. He was glad Pete was silent. If he
heard one more person say "Hot enough for you?," he would just have to
punch him out. The only thing worse than the heat was the fact that he had
to get out there in the field and work in it. And he was in no mood to hear
these fools who didn't know what it was like to be out there sweatin' all day
talk cute about the heat.

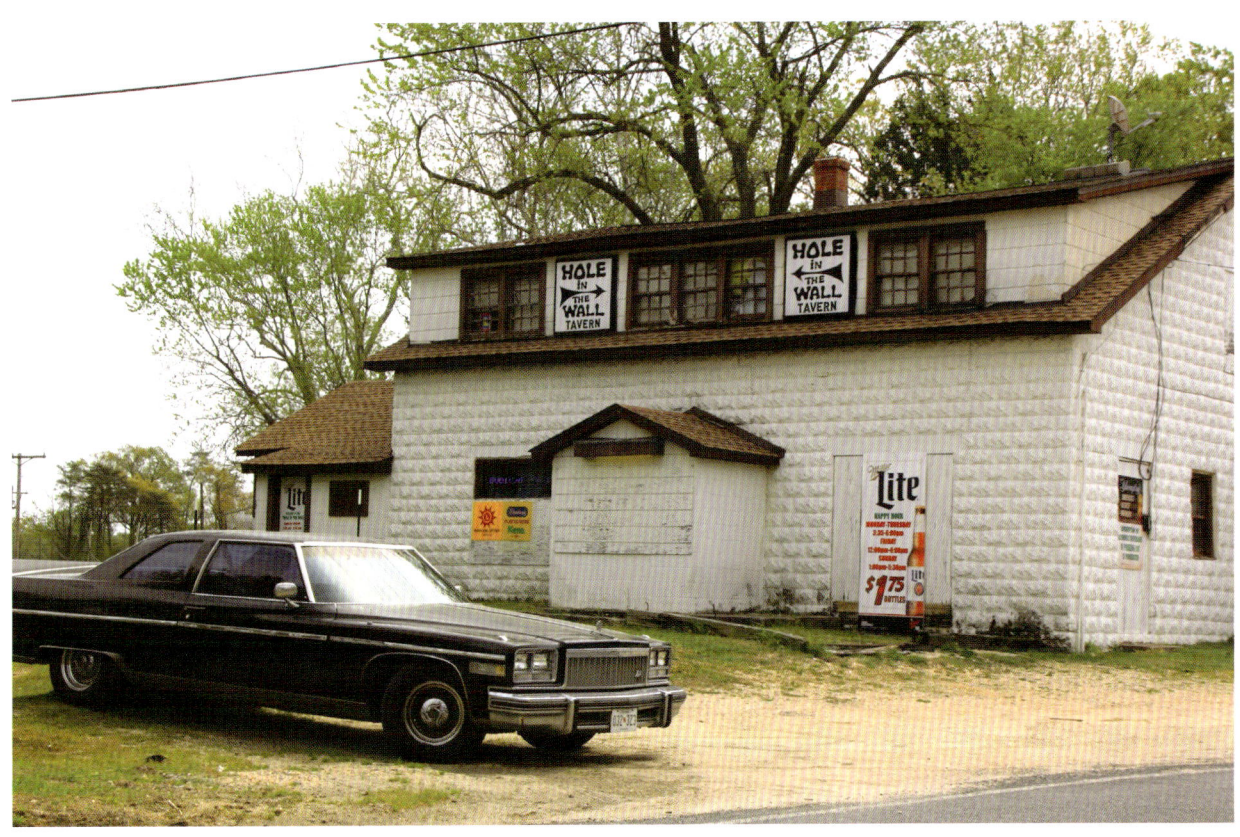

Tavern on Sotterley Road in Hollywood.

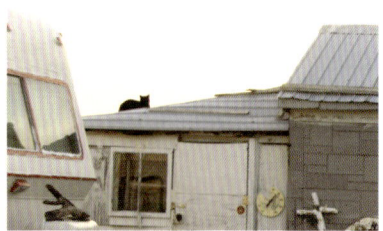

Here kitty? Kitty-cat? Now, where's that darn cat
got to? Robert, have you seen the kitty?

THE LAST HE'D SEEN OF THAT LITTLE DEVIL, she was down at the docks, in and out of the boats, freeloading as usual. Robert was of the opinion that the cat was out enjoying the fine evening breeze and would be in when she was ready for her dinner and not before. He was convinced the creature took pleasure in worrying Edna just to stay one-up. There was no doubt who ruled the roost in this house.

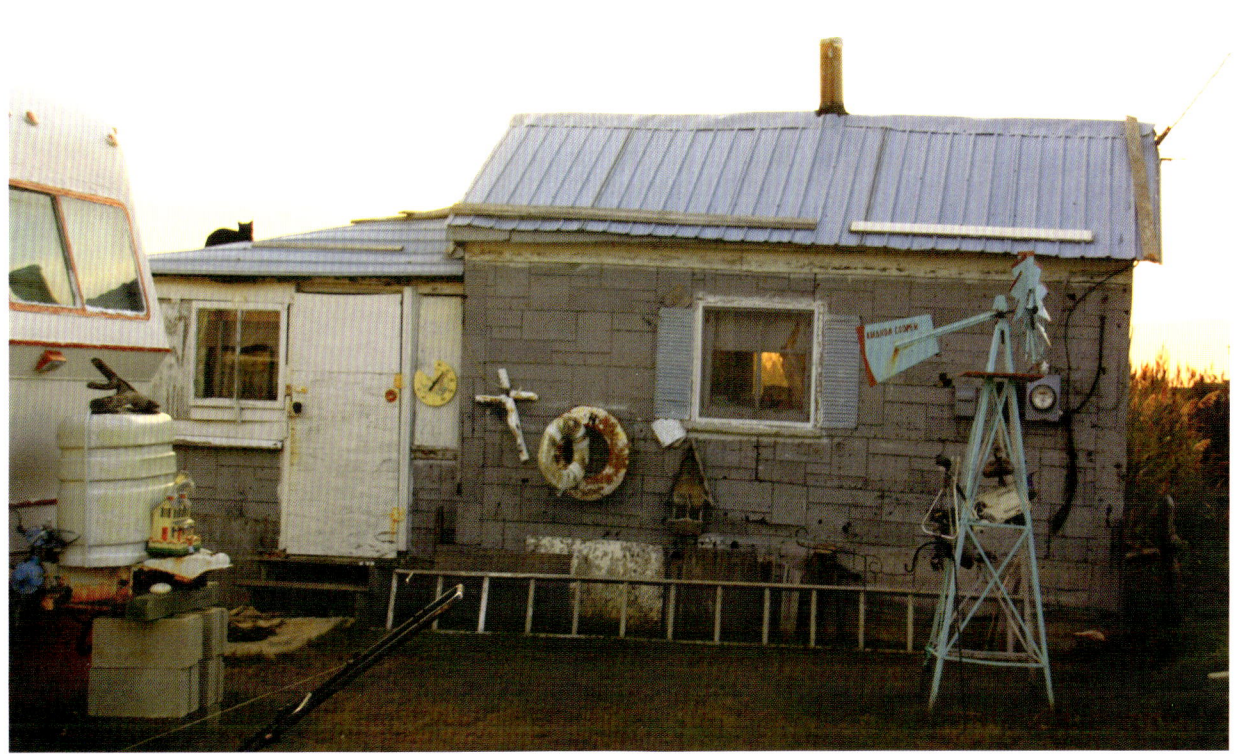

On Chesapeake Bay.

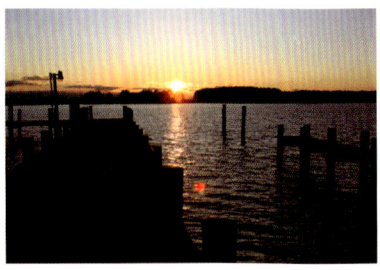

You go on without me, Dad. Maybe tomorrow.

Hᴇ'ᴅ ʙᴇᴇɴ ᴍᴇssɪɴɢ ᴀʙᴏᴜᴛ ɪɴ ʙᴏᴀᴛs since he was a small boy. Started running his dad's boat on Smith Creek when he was ten years old, any chance he got. He'd be out before sun up, checking pound nets or pulling crab pots, and he felt like a man. He could handle himself. Knew just what to do to empty the nets and sometimes free a trapped turtle that got tangled in the net. When he returned from Nam, he had pretty well licked the heroin habit, but he didn't know if he'd ever get back in the boat. He was having pains in his feet and felt like all the strength was just drained out of his legs. Running a boat takes a lot of balance, something two good legs help with a whole lot. And his dad didn't seem to trust him much, not as much as when he was a little kid. He thought he'd get out there on the water, though, just for the ride. Sometime soon. Right now, he felt kind of like one of those sea turtles he used to rescue. But he'd get untangled and come right. Just a matter of time. That's all he needed.

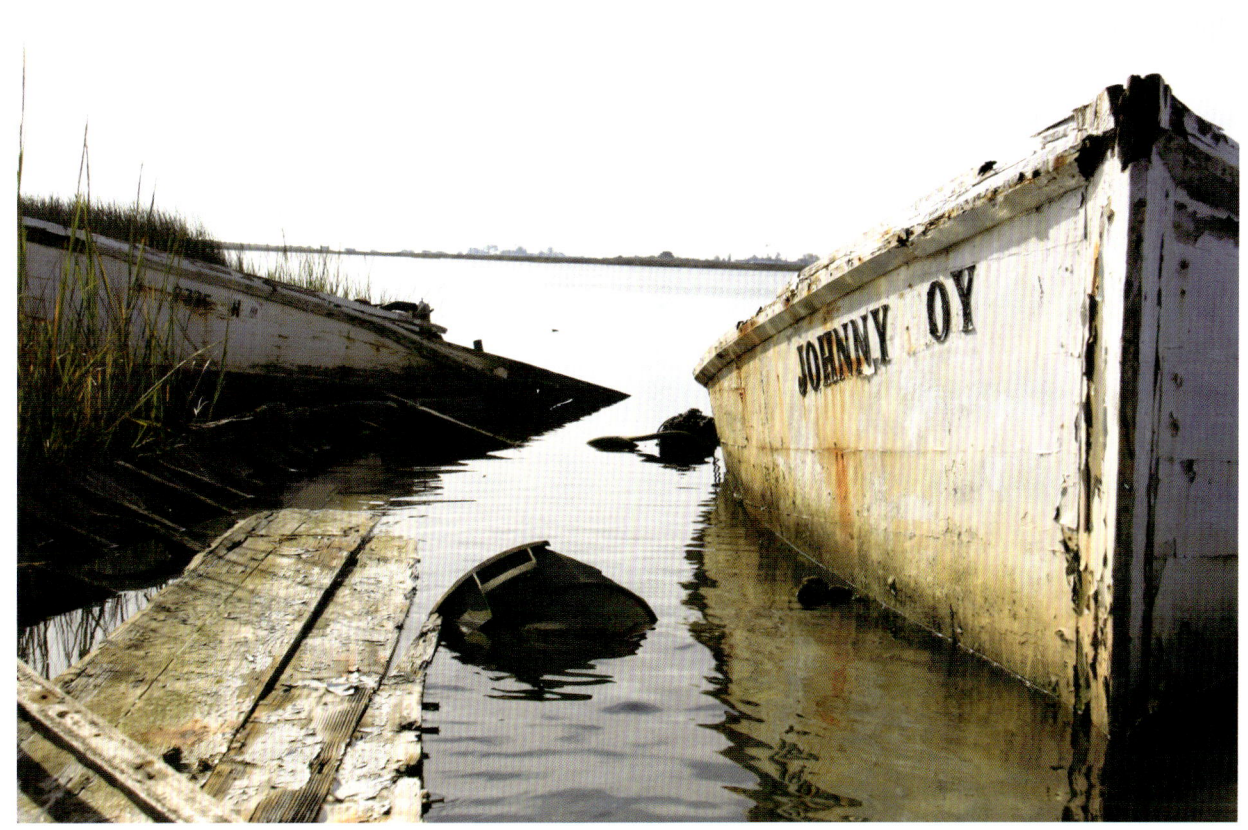

On Chesapeake Bay.

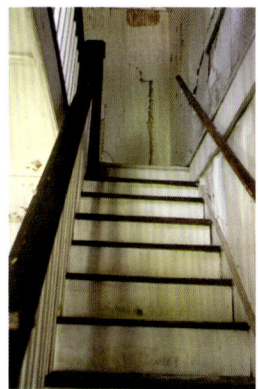

Matthew? Matthew, where are you? I need to get to the chores.

"MA, COME ON NOW. You know Pa's gone, been gone for two years." He spoke gently, hiding the edge of irritation from his voice as best he could. His mother looked up at him, confusion evident on her slack-jawed face. "Matthew?" He couldn't suppress the sigh this time. "No, Ma, it's Luke, your son, Luke." "Oh, that's right," she said, with her vague, embarrassed smile. "I knew that. You're a good boy, Luke." It was becoming more difficult for the family to care for her, but they dreaded letting go, shoving her out the door to be cared for by strangers. She'd shared the house with them since they married. And he had never lived anywhere else, unless you count the time he was at Cape May for Coast Guard training. They'd all got along. And his mother had been a big help when the kids came along. They weren't like a lot of families, spread to the winds and hardly in touch. They hoped they could keep it that way.

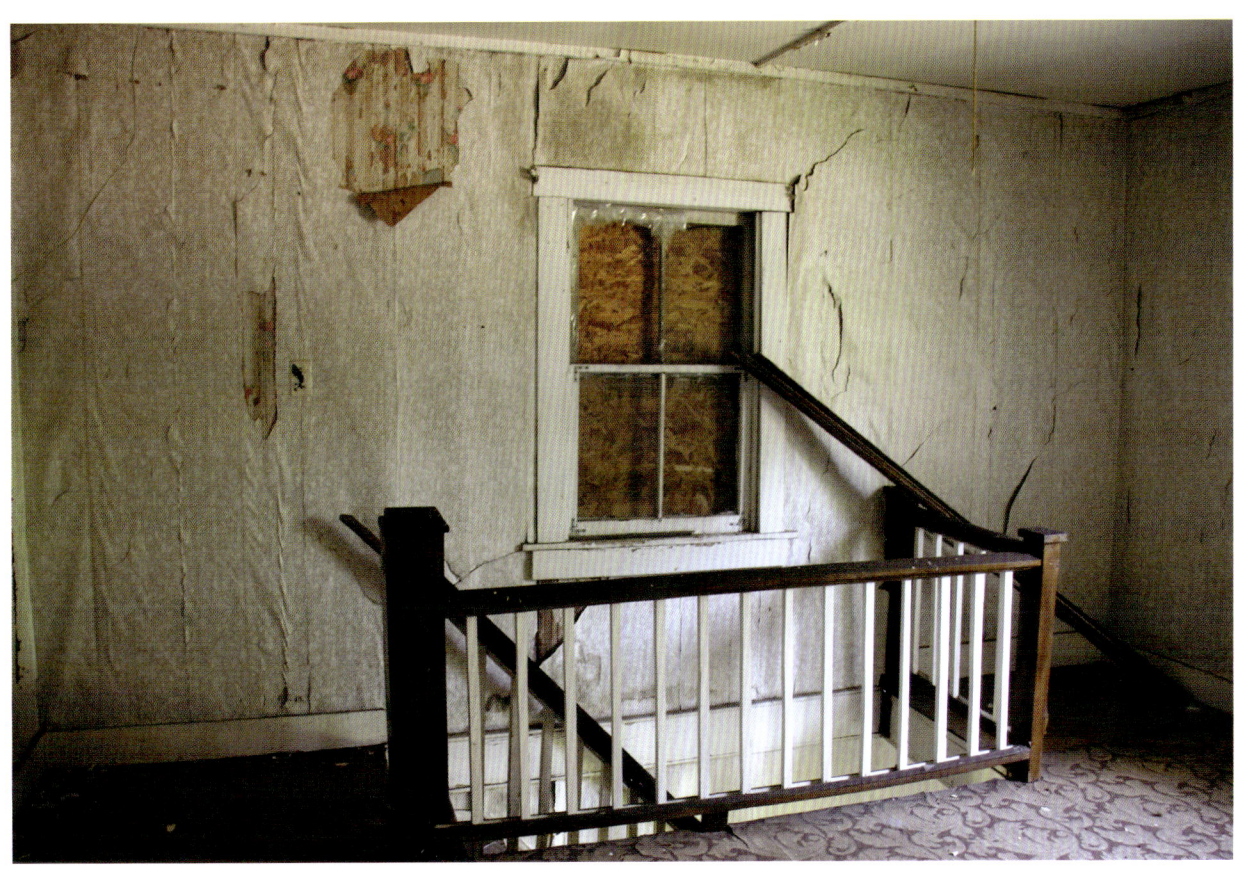

Interior of an old home in Park Hall.

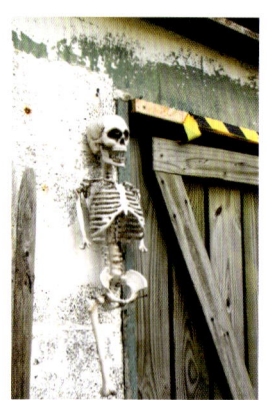

*You folks aren't put off by those old ghost stories are you? You gonna
let silly superstitions get in the way of a good deal like this?*

I T NEVER MATTERED WHAT THE OLD MAN or the realty people he hired said.
No one wanted to take a chance on a house known to have had not just
one but two murders in it. Granted, the first was way back in Civil War times,
so it hardly counted. A black soldier got killed with his own gun by a young
fellow escaped from the Reb prison camp down at Point Lookout. Got away,
too. Took a boat and slipped across the Potomac River to Virginia. That second
one, though, the two brothers. Accident or not, that upset a lot of people.

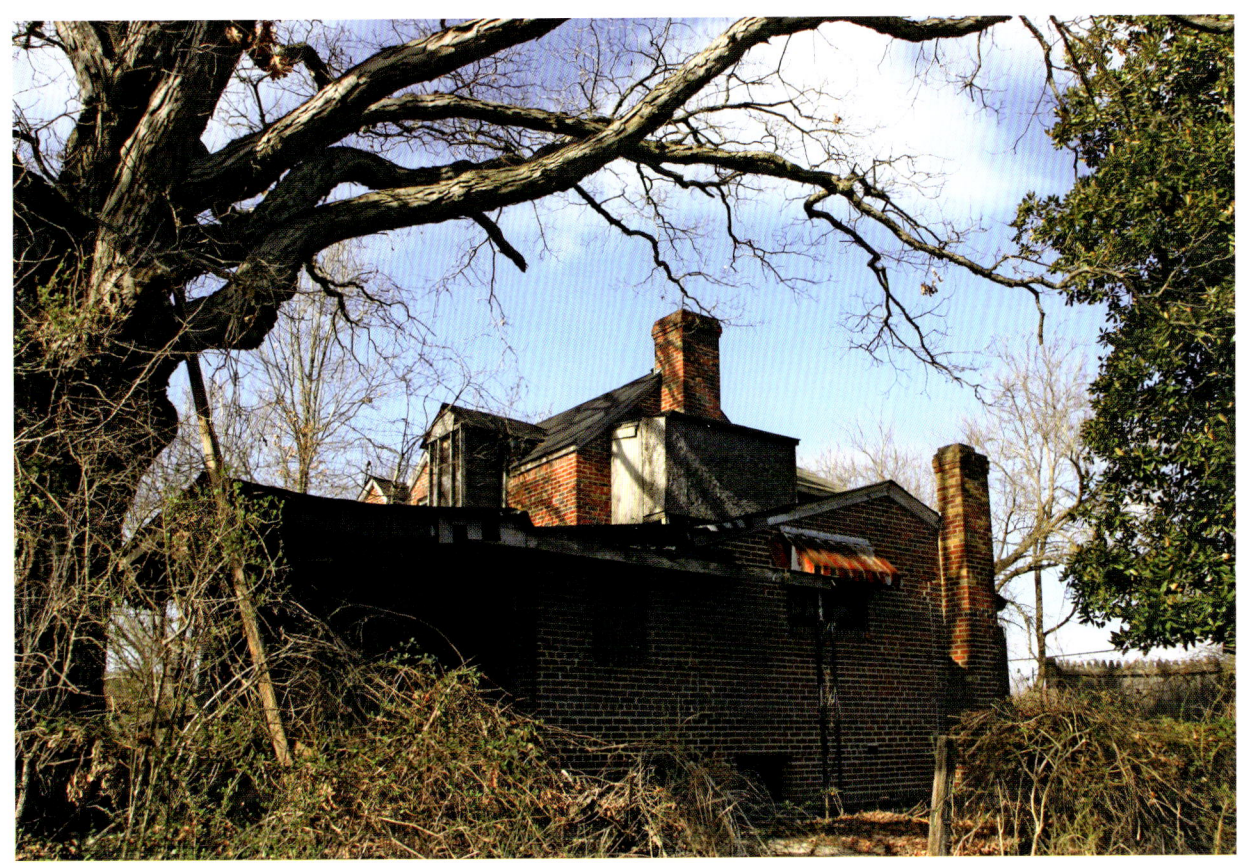

Near Bel Alton.

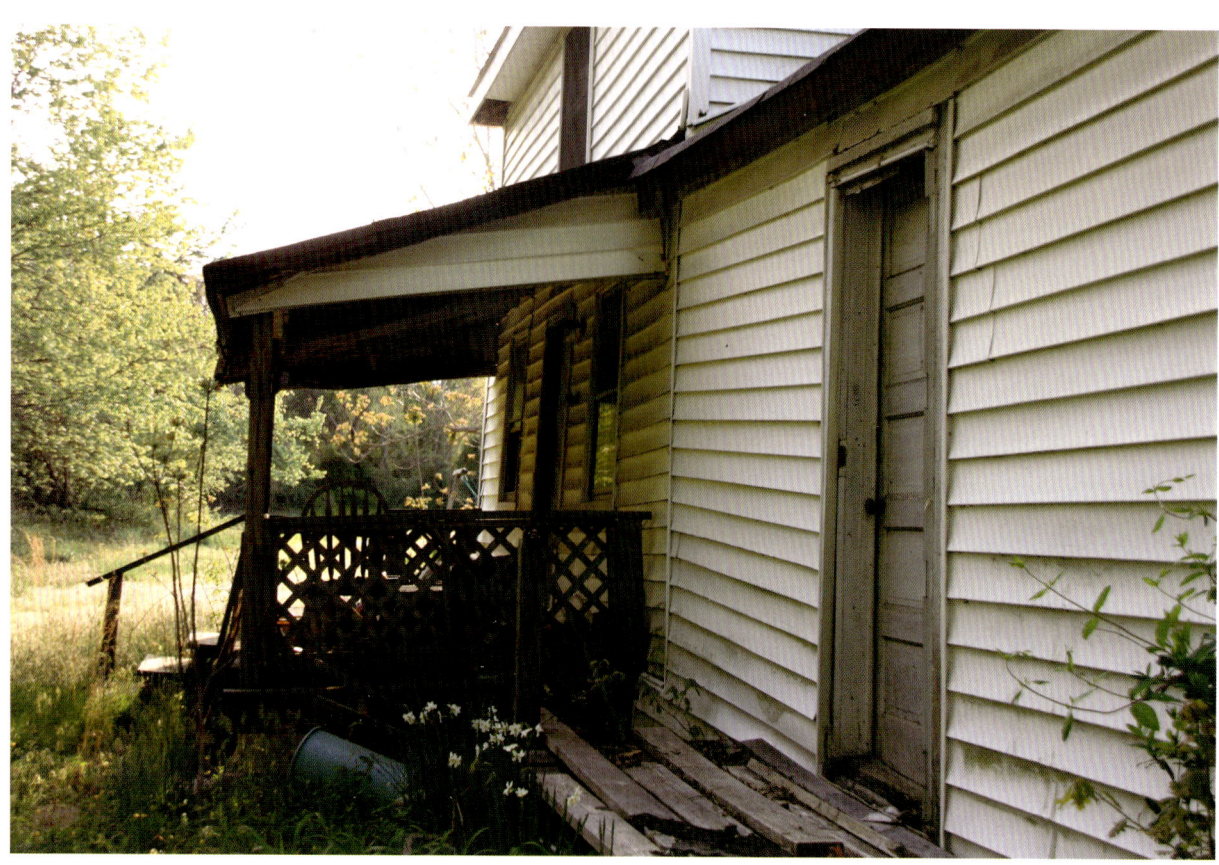

Charlotte Hall.

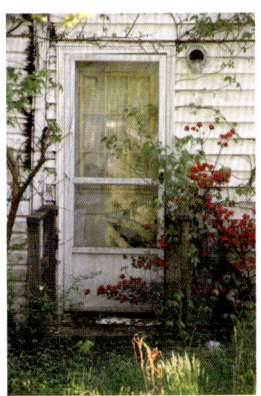

Harrison, could you bring me a little water?
Maybe fluff up this pillow just a bit?

HIS SISTER LAY ON THE NARROW BED by the window where she'd been for three months now and where she'd stay 'til she got so bad they'd take her to the hospital in Charlotte Hall or 'til the end. His big sister. He'd promised her no nursing home no matter what. That was her fear—to be with all those sick old crazy people. Better to be home with family, even if you are stuck in the bed. She wasn't much trouble for the old man, quiet and uncomplaining just like always. Two ladies from the social services came to check on them every few weeks, and he had the girl in to help clean her up. Deacon Somerville came around every week, weather permitting, and that was a comfort. The family was just the two of them now, well three counting the hound. They didn't have much, but they made do.

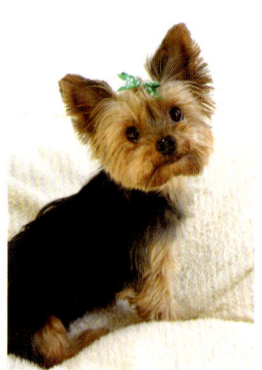

Loretta, hold still, girl! Jerry, pass me that towel and hold on to her while I get Belle up here. The water's getting cold.

IT WAS IMPORTANT TO GET THE PUPS LOOKING THEIR BEST. They would be decked out in full regalia for their moment in the spotlight. Pink and green ribbons lay ready on the dresser. After arguing over the expense, they had purchased a new leash and collar set for both Loretta and Belle. It was hard to keep them groomed and presentable living in the farmhouse. This place was not the mens' first choice, of course, not by a long shot. A townhouse in Fells Point would be more their style, if they could afford it. But Alan's uncle had left him the house, and it was close enough to Baltimore that Jerry could commute to his office there for the few years he had left 'til retirement. They did enjoy the quiet and the room to garden. Work on the old house was an ongoing process. Social life was nil, of course. They didn't like to give their neighbors any more to whisper about if they could help it. The ugly looks they got in the little country market they resorted to when supplies ran low were bad enough. Sometimes, the men felt like aliens from another planet. But they got up to the city and their friends often enough on weekends, and they had the Yorkies, the shows, and each other. They were reasonably happy, they guessed.

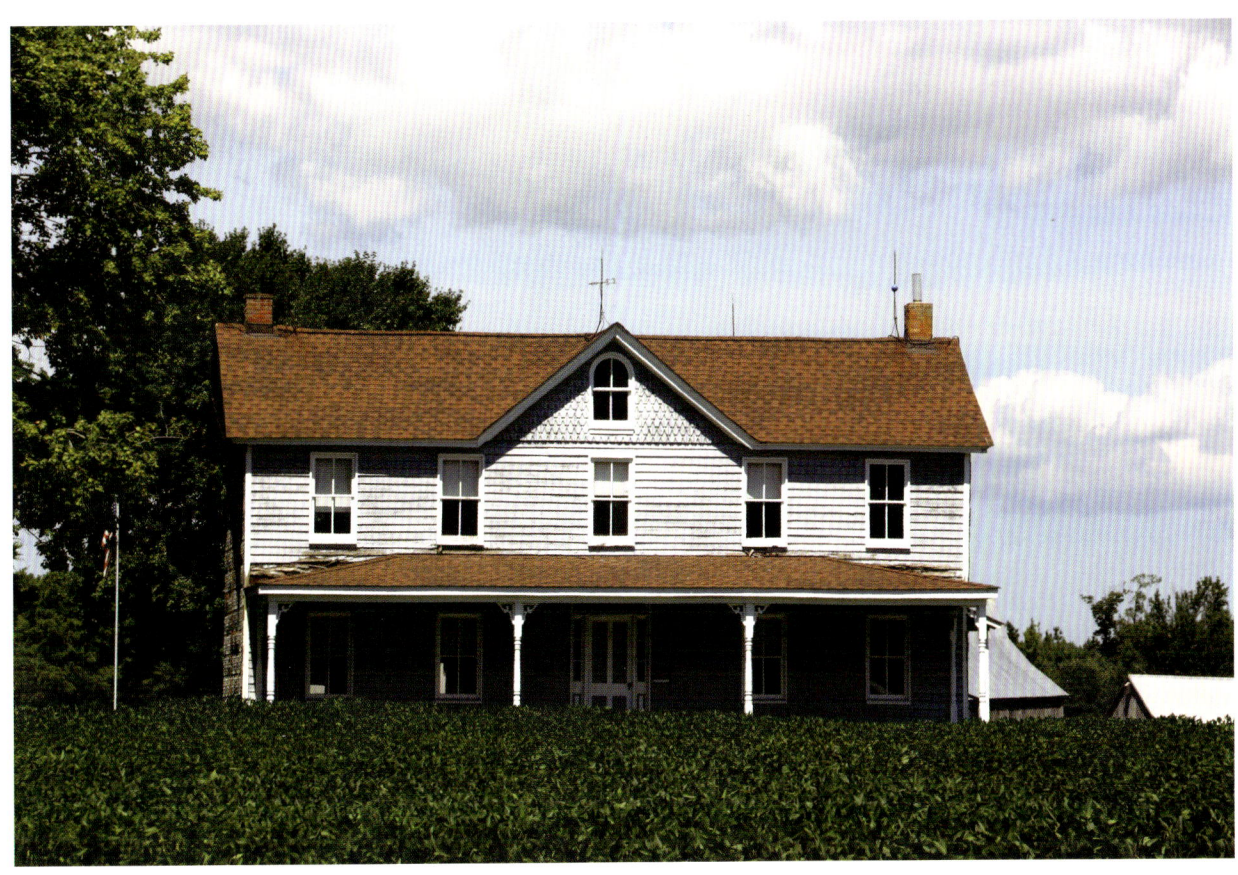

Point Lookout Road.

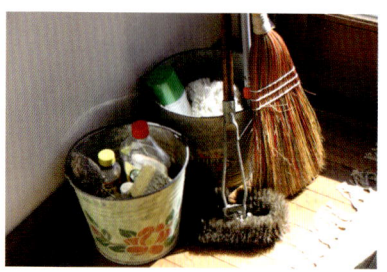

Tommy, let your sister work on that window,
and get up here and help me turn this mattress!

SPRING CLEANING. Tommy and his sister, Jane, dreaded nothing more than the annual ordeal. Their mother attacked the traditional practice with the same zeal she brought to the other religious rituals of the season. With a kerchief tied 'round her head, armed with buckets, mops, sponges, brooms, and solvents of all kinds, she went to war against dirt. The process occupied an entire weekend and wiped out any chance of going out in search of adventures, like exploring the nearby creek or looking for shark's teeth on the beach along the bay. No pick-up baseball game or tag football for Tommy. No reading and visiting with friends on the phone for Jane. "Cleanliness is next to Godliness" wasn't just a proverb in their house; it was a talisman their mother clung to with a grip of steel.

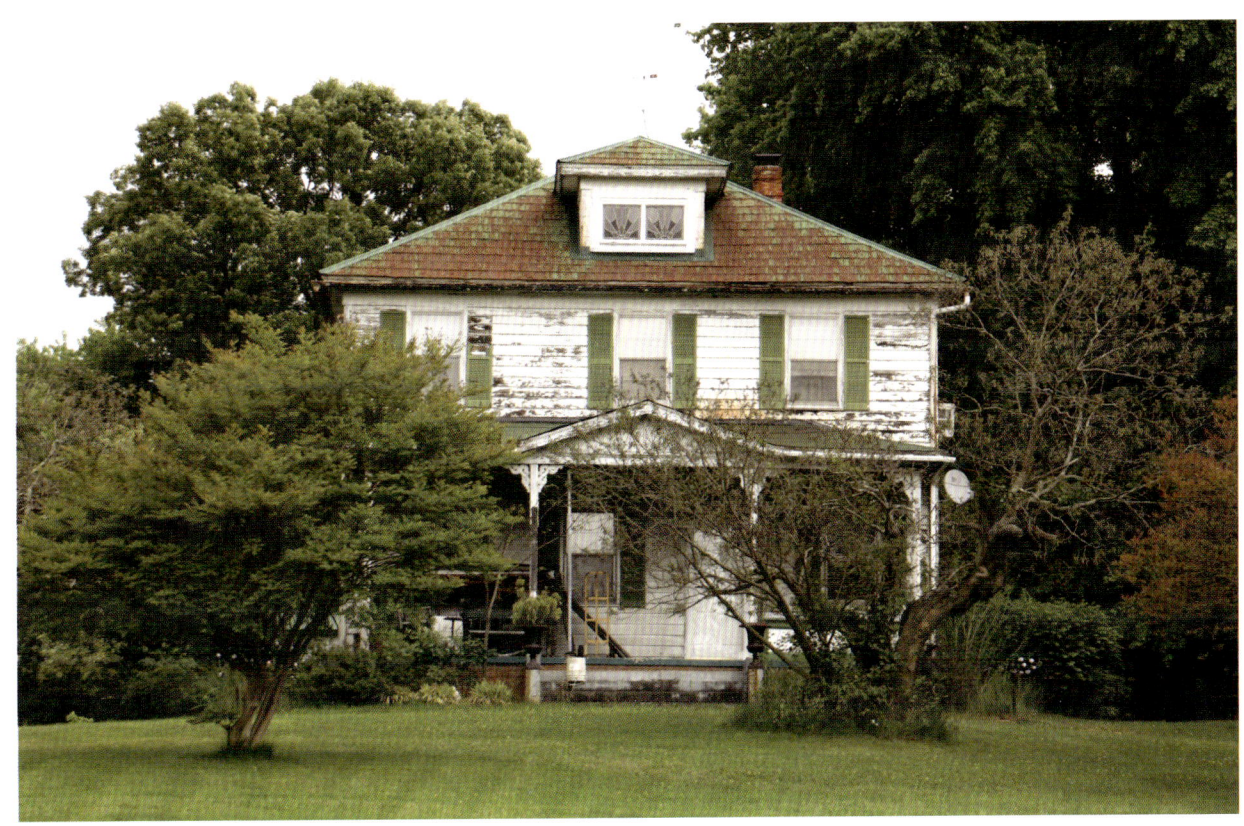

Hughesville.

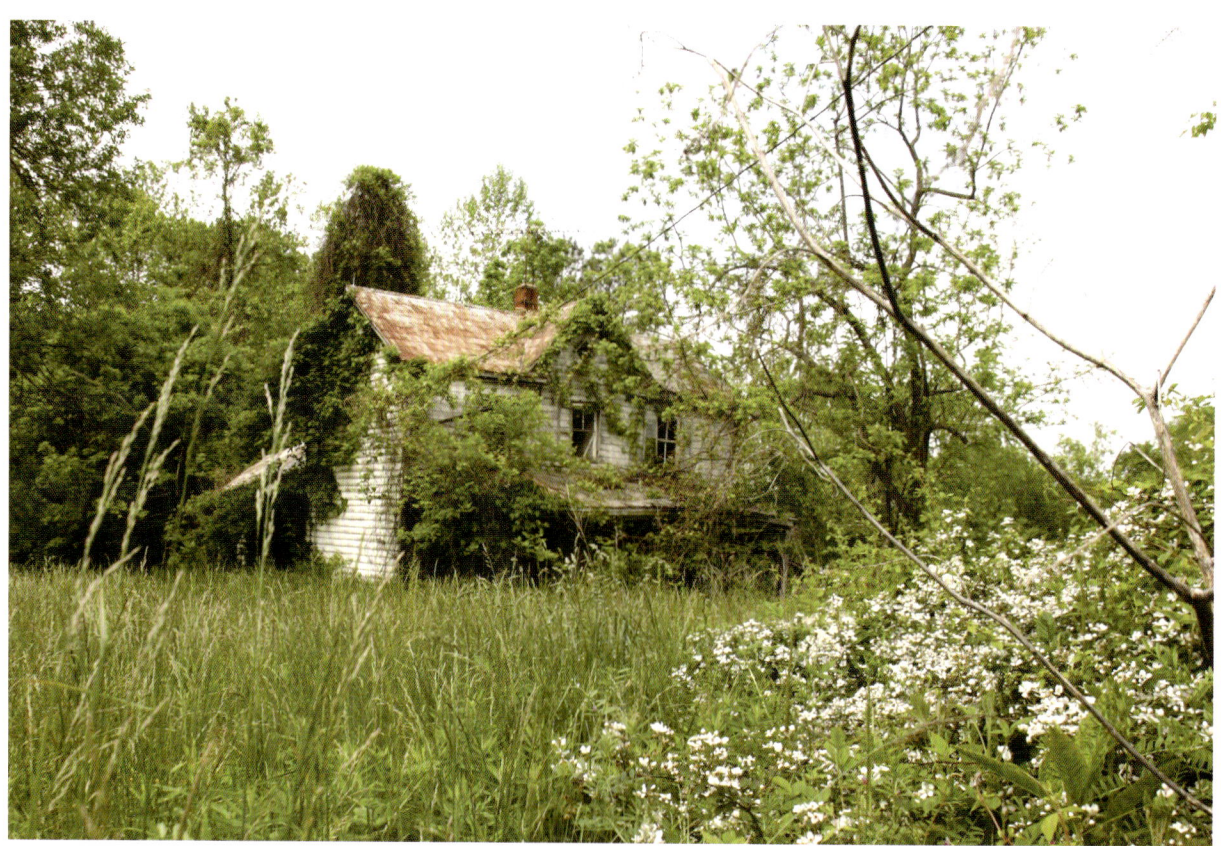

Clements.

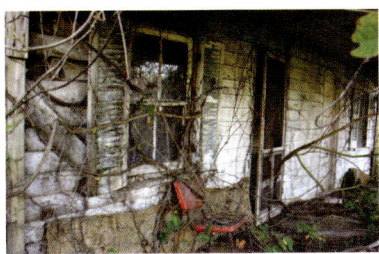

There, your basket is perfect! Now, when you hang it on the door and knock,
be sure and run quick as you can. You don't want to be caught and kissed!

THE LITTLE GIRL'S MOTHER showed her how to make the May Day baskets, folding and cutting the tissue paper so it looked almost like a del-
icate lace bag. She knew such clever ways to do things. And while they sat at
the kitchen table making the baskets together, the mother told her daughter
about the history of May Day baskets and how the tradition went all the way
back to ancient times and the Roman goddess, Flora. That was very much
like Florence, the little girl's name, so she liked that part of the story especially. They put a few nuts and candies in each one and topped them with a
flower. What a smart and altogether wonderful mother she had, thought Florence. They had five fat little baskets when they finished, each with a colorful
flower peeking out the top, ready for the little girl to go hang them on her
friends' front doors and then run like crazy, laughing and half-scared.

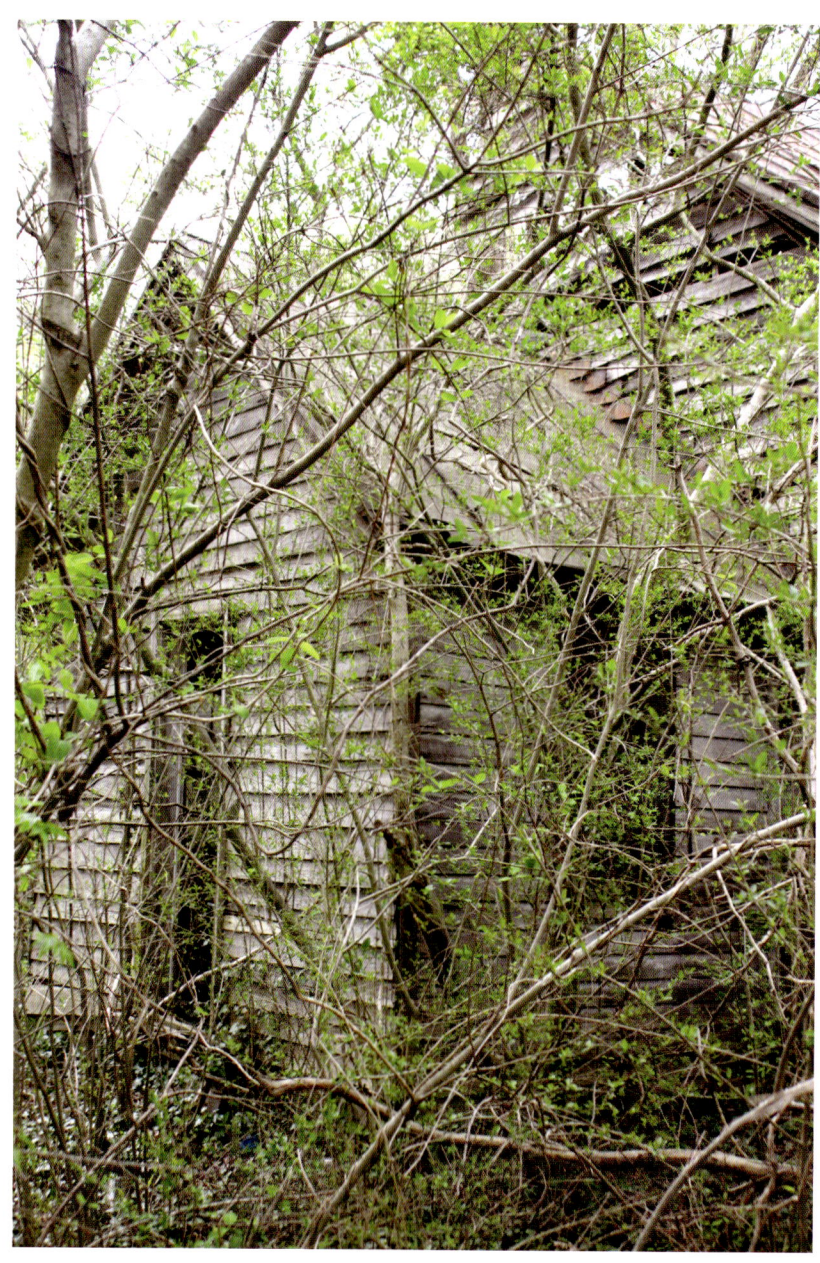

African-American schoolhouse (1896–1940s) in St. Inigoes.

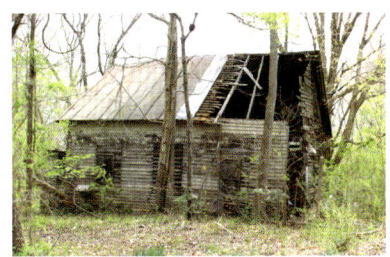

That's the old school there. Someone lived in it
for a while, but it's been empty for some years now.

TESSIE POINTED OUT THE OLD TWO-ROOM BUILDING to her visitor. She had attended the St. Inigoes school through sixth grade but had to come out when her mama got pregnant again and then died having her sister, Ella. Tessie had liked school, but she felt like that was just the way it was. Someone had to stay home. She was glad her brothers and sisters finished school, every one of 'em. They all had babies, too, but Tessie never had babies. She did have a nice husband, and she held him close long as he lived.

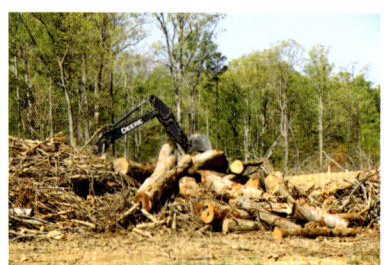

*Babe, have you seen what's happening on Forest Road? They've cut down
all the trees from Bailey's place almost all the way to town!*

LOU FELT LIKE SHE'D BEEN PERSONALLY ASSAULTED when she saw the cleared
lots. She and Becky had figured that the old forest land would likely
be developed at some point. The county was getting carved up fast. But the
suddenness of it jolted her. One minute there was a blanket of forest, and the
next a patch of scraped bare earth with houses already going up. She was still
bothered by the gaping hole left by the tooth she'd had extracted last week,
and the felling of the trees felt to her like yet another loss. She didn't like
what was happening to the county with the developers coming in. She didn't
like people calling it progress. And she didn't appreciate being reminded how
her own body was aging. Change was inevitable, but it was always only good
for some people, and, lately, it wasn't her.

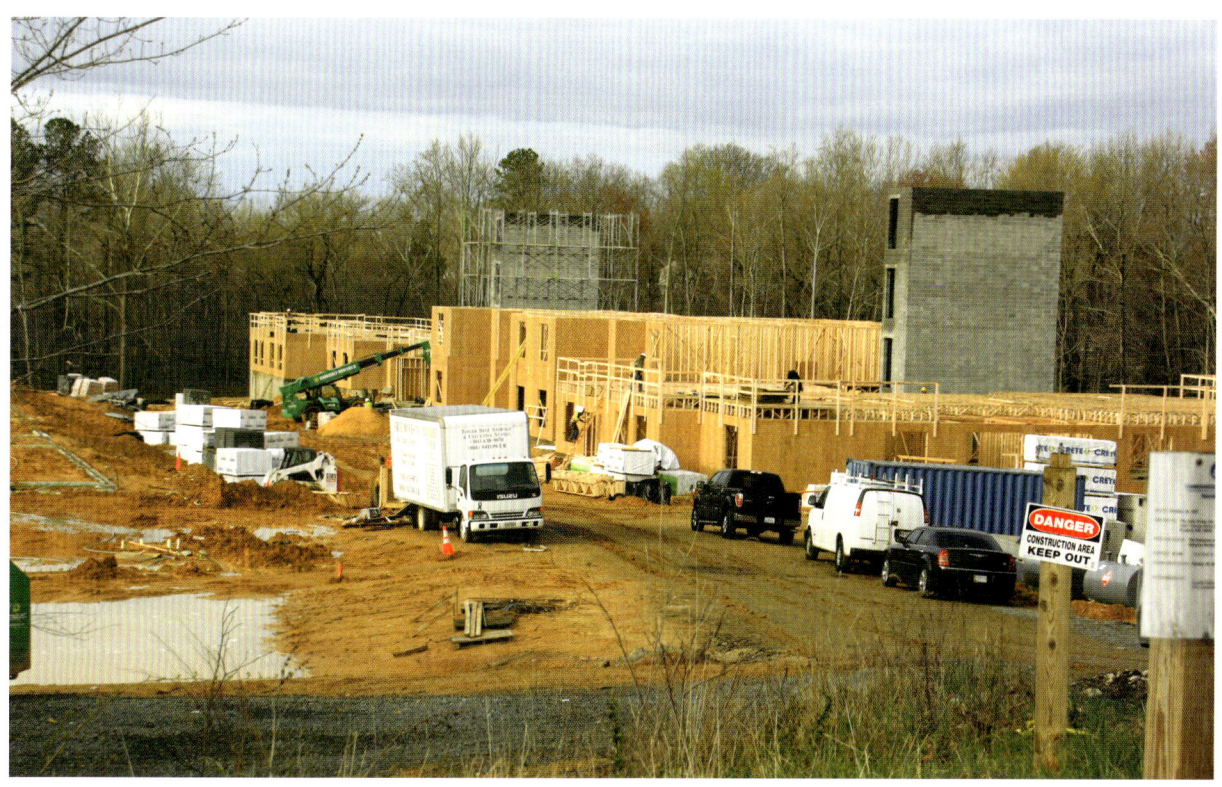

The Hamptons in Leonardtown.

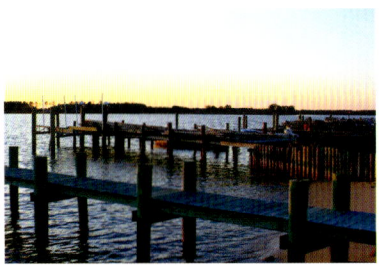

Now, don't forget to save room for some blackberry cobbler.

THEY'D BEEN COMING HERE FOR YEARS, bringing the boat down from Annapolis on a Saturday or Sunday afternoon, but they'd never brought this strange, silent grandchild with them. She sat there with her chopped hair and black lipstick, eating her fried oysters with no sign of enjoyment or any other emotion that they could detect. They felt at sea, not knowing even how to make her feel that they cared. And they did care about her, just as they cared about her mother who hadn't really talked to them in years. As busy as they were enjoying their "golden years," they felt they had lost some vital connection to what mattered, and no amount of boat trips, good food, or summer vacations would help them find it again.

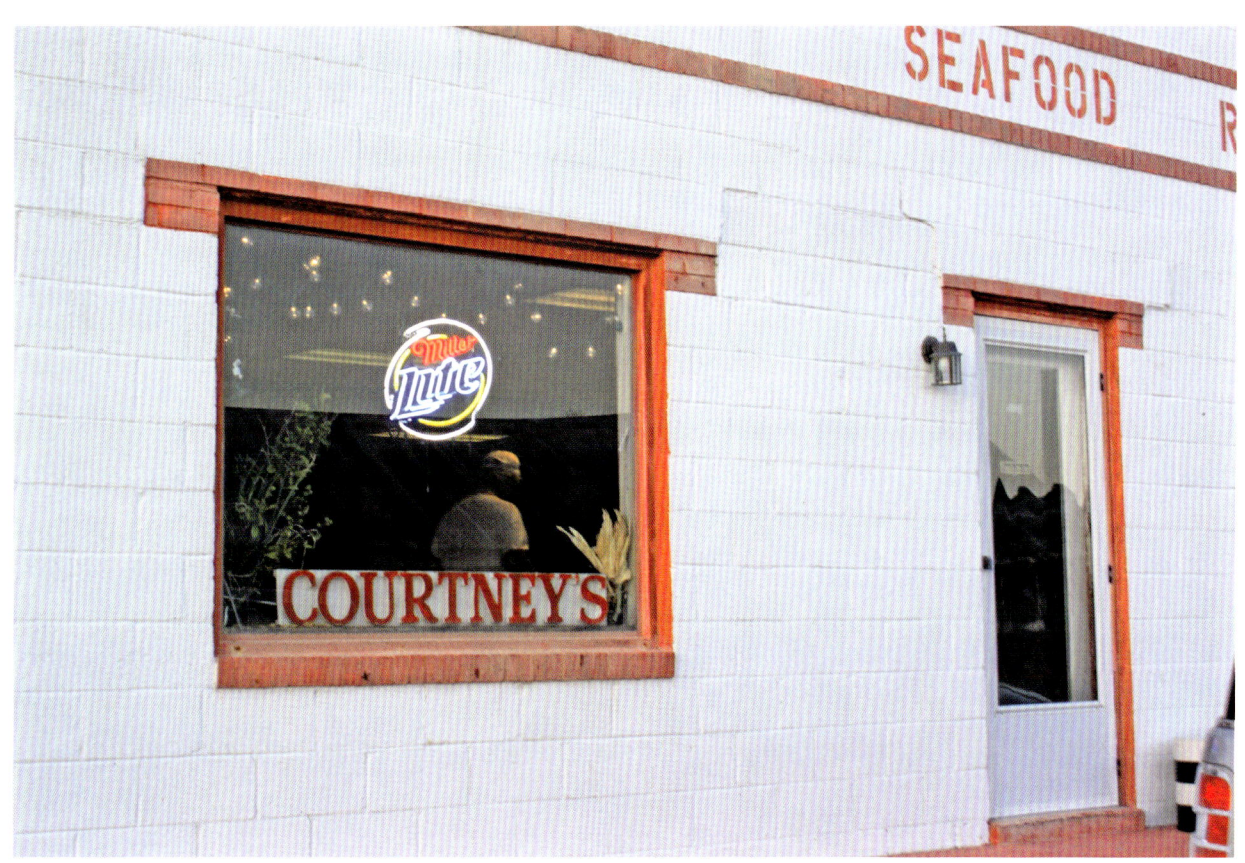

Courtney's on Smith Creek.

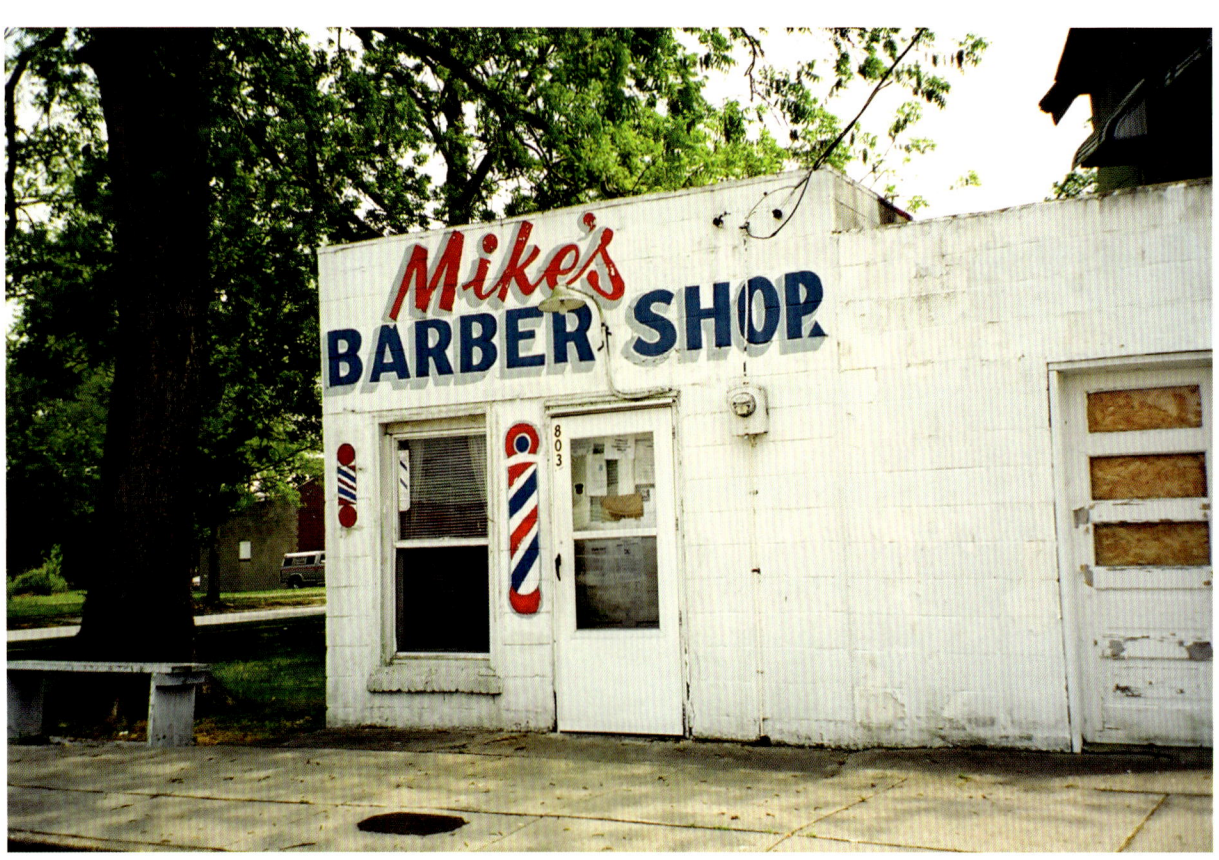

Mike's backroad barber shop.

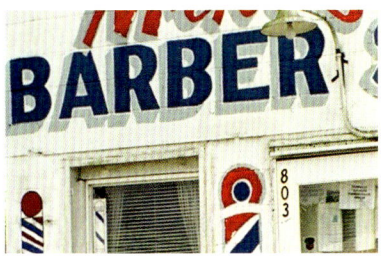

Just do the usual. I don't need no fancy hieroglyphics
carved in there like these young kids got.

V ERNON SAT BACK IN THE CHAIR as Mike adjusted the cape, picked up the clippers, and continued his epic tale of Saturday-night drama in the neighborhood. "So she was acting all cute and everything, those bunny teeth stickin' out one way and her big butt the other, and that boy just grabbed her. I'm not sayin' he wasn't provoked, but that's just no way for a grown man to act now, is it?" The two customers waiting on the worn, red vinyl chairs assured him it was not. Vernon just mumbled and gave a half-smile, lost in replaying memories of his own Saturday and how it had left him with the undeniable fact that he had a pregnant teenage daughter on his hands, a boiling-mad wife who had managed to find a way to blame him somehow, and a certain knowledge that he was not up to the task of dealing with any of it to the satisfaction of the women in his life.

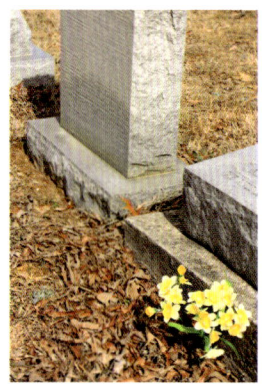

Yea, when this flesh and heart shall fail,
And mortal life shall cease,
I shall possess, within the veil,
A life of joy and peace.
—From "Amazing Grace" by John Newton (1779)

Miss Mary loved singing "Amazing Grace," and she loved being in church. She used to go to the big church in Busy Corner, but she liked visiting the small churches around the county, especially on their Homecoming days, and she didn't care what denomination it was. They were all good folk, and being there made her feel like she was part of something bigger, friendly, and uplifting. Like everything was right with the world. When she went to the big church, she still sat in the back, even though she didn't have to anymore. She didn't mind. She wouldn't feel comfortable making trouble. Let other folks get upset. She was just glad to be there.

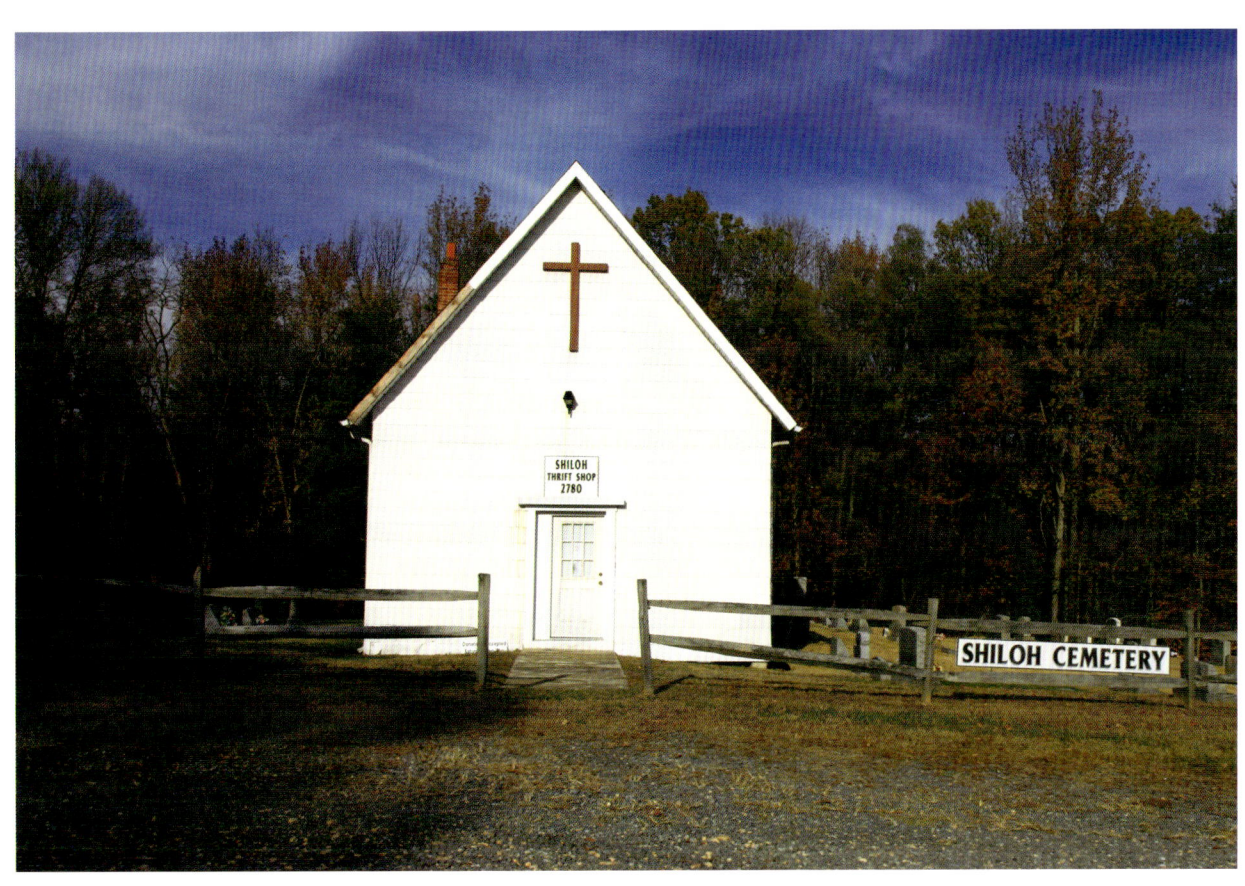

Shiloh Cemetery on Bryans Road.

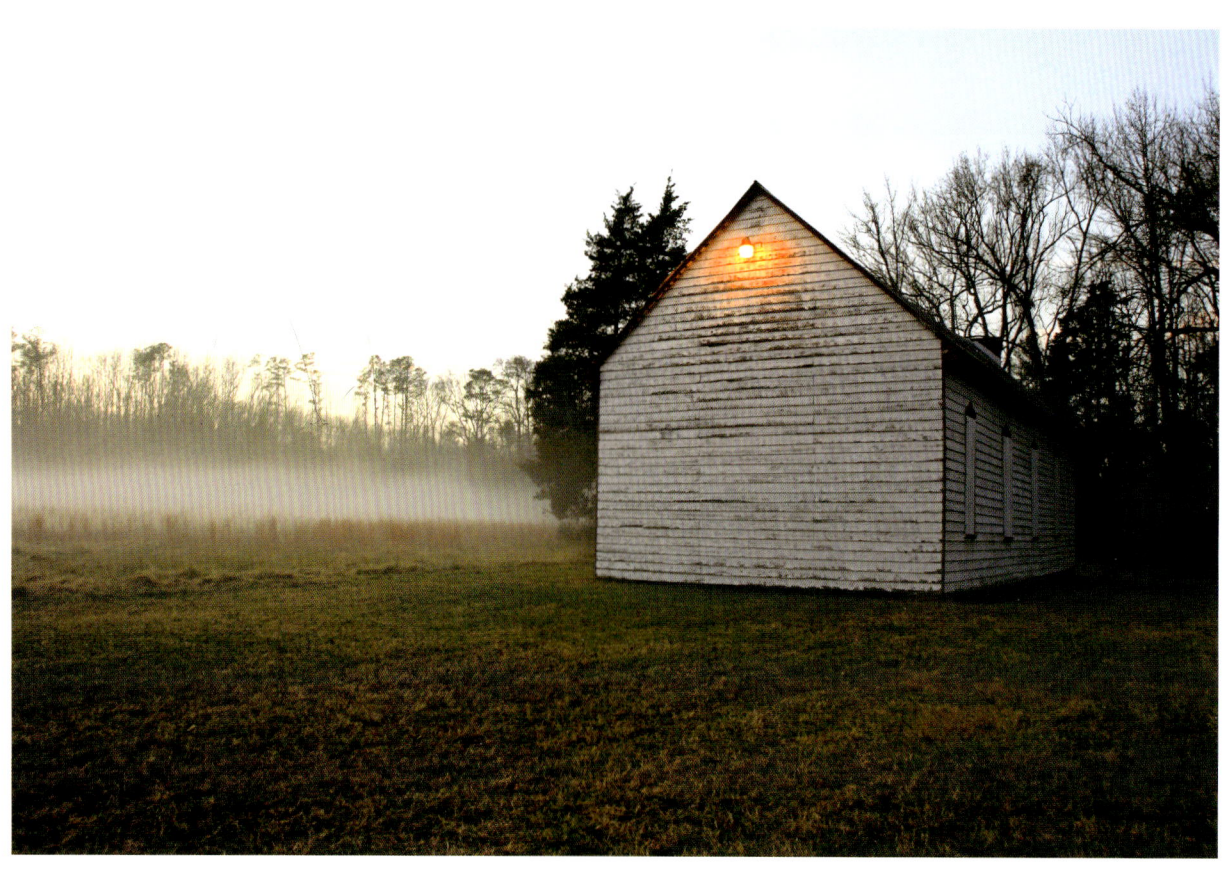

Old Holy Face Church (1887) in Great Mills.

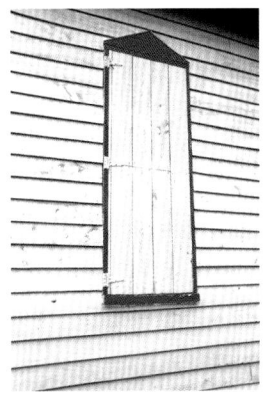

We are gathered together . . .

STANDING NEAR THE BAPTISMAL FONT, Michael's eyes focused on a small imperfection in the embroidery on the baby's white gown. The sun had broken through the clouds, and the late-afternoon light coming through the west window revealed the pulled threads just below the collar. The baptismal gown had been handed down through the family since it was fashioned by his grand-aunt, Agnes, with fabric from her mother's wedding gown. A shaft of sunlight suddenly lit up the whole gown and the drops of water falling on his grandson's forehead. The light seemed to him a sign that the hope and promise this new life had brought him was supported by the universe.

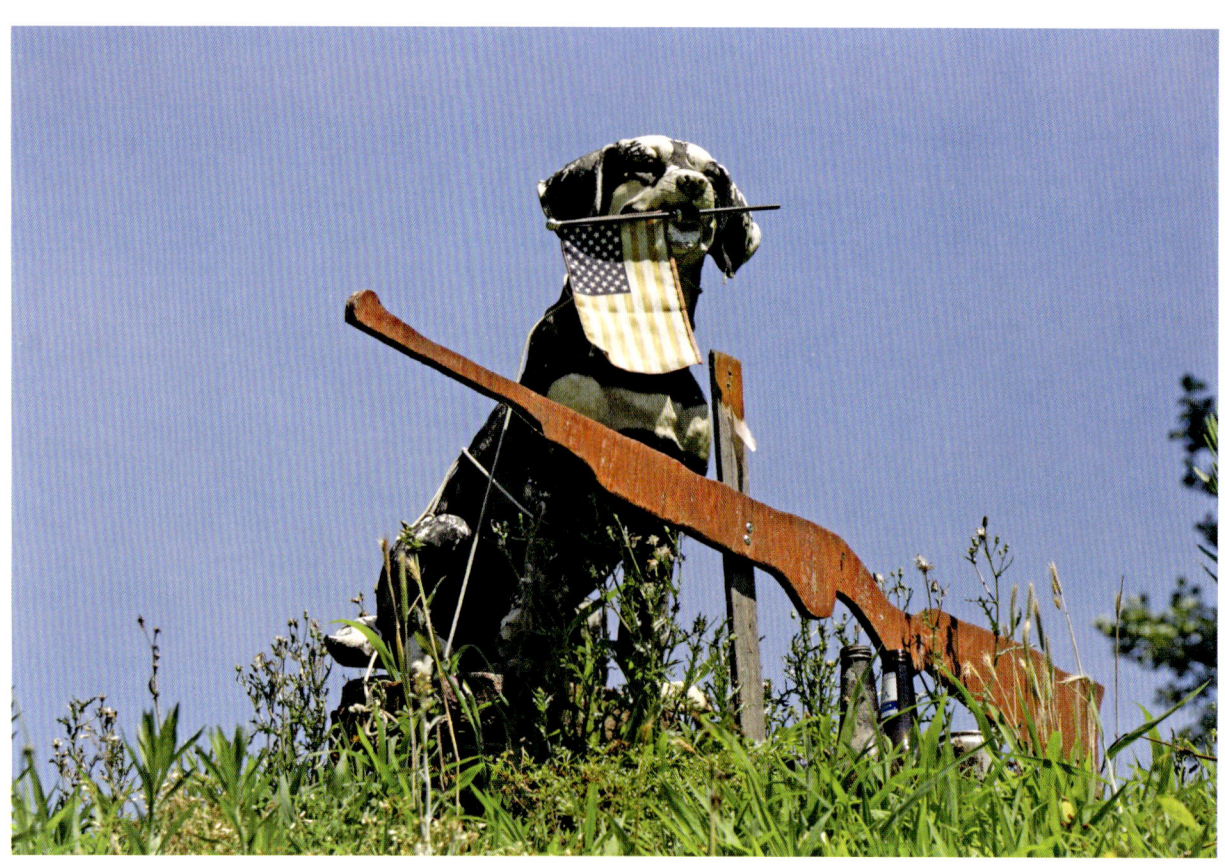

Roadside sculpture in Valley Lee.

Acknowledgments

I AM EXTREMELY FORTUNATE to be supported by friends and colleagues who are generous with their time and talents. I am especially grateful to Jacqueline Paskow and Faith Potts, dear friends who helped me immeasurably with this project by applying their sharp eyes and substantial editing talents to my many drafts. I am deeply grateful, as well, to Alma Thompson Jordon, my friend and companion on many enjoyable excursions scouting backroads for photo-worthy sites. She and the whole wonderful Thompson family shared their history, served as readers, and helped out in myriad other ways, including serving as models in the photo that appears on page 56. My colleagues at St. Mary's College—Karen Leona Anderson, Jeffrey Coleman, and Jeffrey Hammond—offered support and encouragement at critical junctures as well, and I am graeful for Jeff's foreword. Thank you to Julie King, Meghan Webster, Chelsey Ganse and Bella, Christina Allen, and Jane Rowe, for helping along the way. George Thompson's enthusiasm and inspiring editorial guidance were essential in bringing this project to fruition as a book. And thanks also to Mikki Soroczak, for her editorial assistance, and to David Skolkin, for his elegant book design. As always, the support of my partner, Bob Lewis, has been indispensible.

I express my appreciation, too, for my colleagues in the Unified Committee for Afro-American Contributions of St. Mary's County, Historic Sotterley Plantation, Inc., and the St. Mary's College of Maryland Slackwater Center. All three organizations are doing the important work of collecting local oral histories. Last but not least, I thank the people of St. Mary's County who shared their stories so that the history of how we have lived is not lost and can be passed on to all who wish to listen in.

About the Essayist

Jeffrey Hammond is George B. and Willma Reeves Distinguished Professor in the Liberal Arts and Professor of English at St. Mary's College of Maryland. He has published three scholarly books, most recently *The American Puritan Elegy: A Literary and Cultural Study* (Cambridge University Press, 2000), and his books of nonfiction include *Ohio States: A Twentieth-Century Midwestern* (Kent State University Press, 2002), *This Place Where We Are* (St. Mary's Press, 2006), *Small Comforts: Essays at Middle Age* (Kent State University Press, 2008), and *Little Big World: Collecting Louis Marx and the American Fifties* (University of Iowa Press, 2010). He has won two Pushcart Prizes, been awarded *Shenandoah*'s Carter Prize for the Essay and *The Missouri Review* Editors' Prize for the Essay, and his literary nonfiction appeared in such journals as *American Scholar, Antioch Review, Fourth Genre, Gettysburg Review, Hotel Amerika, Ohio Magazine, River Styx, River Teeth, Southern Review, Under the Sun*, and *Virginia Quarterly Review*.

About the Author

Merideth Taylor is Professor Emerita of Theater and Dance in the Department of Theater, Film, and Media Studies at St. Mary's College of Maryland in Historic St. Mary's City. She has a broad and eclectic background in theater and dance as a performer, director, choreographer, and teacher. She was honored by the St. Mary's County Branch of the NAACP with a Lifetime Achievement Award for her use of the performing arts to produce positive social change. As a writer, Taylor has received awards in playwriting, screenwriting, and historical documentation. Her plays have been produced in venues in Washington, D.C., and New York City and selected for readings as far afield as Valdez, Alaska. She received a 2007 Maryland African-American Heritage Preservation Award and a 2007 Historic Preservation Service Award for the book, *In Relentless Pursuit of an Education: African-American Stories from a Century of Segregation* (Unified Committee for Afro-American Contributions of St. Mary's County, 2006), which she co-edited. Among Taylor's recent projects, she has served as the lead writer on "Land, Lives, and Labor," an award-winning permanent exhibit mounted by Historic Sotterley Plantation in Hollywood, Maryland, and as Project Director on Sotterley's National Institute of Library and Museum Studies grant-funded "Engaging Audiences" Reinterpretation project. She received a 2010 Historic Preservation Service Award from the St. Mary's County Historic Preservation Committee and County Commissioners for the documentary, *With All Deliberate Speed: One High School's Story*, and, in 2011, a Communicators International Award for her short film, *Historic Sotterley: A Tidewater Legacy.* The films were selected for inclusion and awards in the 2016 and 2017 Southern Maryland Film Festivals. She shares a homestead in Park Hall, Maryland, with her partner, Bob, two cats, and a small flock of chickens.

About the Craft

I TOOK THE PHOTOGRAPHS over a period of many years, during which time I made the transition from a Nikon Lite Touch Zoom 150 film camera to a Canon EOS digital Rebel XTi. All shots were taken with natural light and a hand-held camera. During the years I spent traveling southern Maryland's roads, I was not always paying strict attention to crossing county lines, and, though all but a few of the sites photographed are, or were, within St. Mary's county lines, there are a few outliers. I hope that readers will find all images acceptable representations of the local culture. As I started to work on the book, I branched out from images of buildings and began to add constructed or "staged" shots in order to better illustrate the stories. The text incorporates my experience in conducting and editing oral histories and my work as a playwright who draws on local history.

About the Book

Listening In: Echoes and Artifacts from Maryland's Mother Country was brought to publication in an edition of 1,000 hardcover copies. The text was set in Bembo, the paper is Gold East, 157 gsm weight, and the book was professionally printed and bound by P. Chan & Edward, Inc., in China.

Publisher: George F. Thompson
Editorial and Research Assistant: Mikki Soroczak
Manuscript Editor: Purna Makaram
Book Design and Production: David Skolkin

Credit: Lucille Clifton's famous poem, "mulberry fields" (page 7), first appeared in her book, *Mercy* (Rochester, NY: BOA Editions, 2004), 24, and it was reprinted in *The Collected Poems of Lucille Clifton* 1965–2010, edited by Kevin Young and Michael S. Glaser, with a foreword by Toni Morrison (Rochester, NY: BOA Editions, 2012), 582. Copyright 2004 Lucille Clifton and reprinted with the permission of The Permissions Company, Inc., on behalf of BOA Editions, Ltd. (www.boaeditions.org).

Published 2018. First hardcover edition.
Printed in China on acid-free paper.

George F. Thompson Publishing, L.L.C.
217 Oak Ridge Circle
Staunton, VA 24401–3511, U.S.A.
www.gftbooks.com

26 25 24 23 22 21 20 19 18   1 2 3 4 5

The Library of Congress Preassigned Control Number is 2017919084.

ISBN: 978–1–938086–55–7